THE LITTLE BOOK OF KNOWLEDGE:

NEW HOLLYWOOD

Become our fan on Facebook **facebook.com/idwpublishing**
Follow us on Twitter **@idwpublishing**
Subscribe to us on YouTube **youtube.com/idwpublishing**
See what's new on Tumblr **tumblr.idwpublishing.com**
Check us out on Instagram **instagram.com/idwpublishing**

ISBN: 978-1-68405-068-0

21 20 19 18 1 2 3 4

Greg Goldstein, President & Publisher
Robbie Robbins, EVP & Sr. Art Director
Matthew Ruzicka, CPA, Chief Financial Officer
David Hedgecock, Associate Publisher
Lorelei Bunjes, VP of Digital Services
Jerry Bennington, VP of New Product Development
Eric Moss, Sr. Director, Licensing & Business Development

Ted Adams, Founder & CEO of IDW Media Holdings

Created for Editions Du Lombard by David Vandermeulen and
Nathalie Van Campenhoudt.
Original layout by Elhadi Yazi, Eric Laurin, and Rebekah Paulovich.

THE LITTLE BOOK
OF KNOWLEDGE:

NEW HOLLYWOOD

WRITTEN BY
JEAN-BAPTISTE THORET

ART BY
BRÜNO

TRANSLATION BY
EDWARD GAUVIN

EDITS BY
JUSTIN EISINGER AND ALONZO SIMON

COLLECTION DESIGN BY
RON ESTEVEZ

PUBLISHER:
GREG GOLDSTEIN

THE U.S. CONSENSUS

Is there anyone alive today who hasn't heard of Dirty Harry Callahan, Bonnie Parker, or Don Corleone? Is anything as universally acclaimed today as American movies of the 1970s? One wonders if posterity will find lolcat videos more divisive. The widespread approval that New Hollywood enjoys has become such an impressive phenomenon that it's hard to find a critic working today who would dare admit to being uninterested in the works of George Romero or Don Siegel. Soon enough—if it hasn't happened already—every last turkey in the catalogue of that tried-and-true veteran Mel Brooks will be anointed as a classic. If this unanimous support for New Hollywood seems matter-of-course today, it wasn't always the case. Far from it. A few fans can still remember how, for almost two decades—from the second half of the '80s, when New Hollywood was officially pronounced dead, to the early 2000s—practically no one was into New Hollywood.

It's easy to forget, but the very label "New Hollywood" didn't make it to France until 2002. Truth be told, it happened a bit by chance, when translator Alexandra Peyre took it upon herself to change the title of the first major book on the topic, Peter Biskind's *Easy Riders, Raging Bulls: How the Sex-Drugs-and-Rock-'n'-Roll generation saved Hollywood*, to *The New Hollywood: Coppola, Lucas, Scorsese, Spielberg — The Revolution of a Generation*[1]. Before Biskind's famous work appeared in 2002 (the original had been published in the U.S. in 1998), the phrase "New Hollywood" was entirely unknown in France. More astonishing still than the label and its use, or lack thereof, was how almost no one for more than twenty years ever brought up the emblematic movies of that generation of *enfant terribles*. A generation of filmmakers[2] that—apart from the rare exceptions like Scorsese, Spielberg, or Eastwood, who'd managed to survive four decades of cinema by adapting more or less nimbly to the times—had largely been decimated on the altar of Reagan-era movies. For the entire 1980s, the films of Sam Peckinpah, Don Siegel, and John Frankenheimer were, when not outright impossible to get a hold of, at best seen by the era's intellectuals as second-rate work, unworthy of serious criticism, video store fodder. In fact, the only French critics to appreciate and comment on New Hollywood movies were those writing for "genre" magazines such as *L'Écran fantastique* [Screen Fantasy], *Mad Movies*, or *Starfix*, anti-establishment publications careful to distance themselves from the stuffy academic style with which *Cahiers du Cinéma* and *Positif*[3] occasionally aligned themselves. This lack of interest in New Hollywood was so flagrant and pervasive that it wasn't until the December 1992 issue of *Cahiers du Cinéma*, in an article by Jean-François Rauger (at the time, Rauger had just taken over programming at the Cinémathèque française), that an establishment voice dared invoke the name of 1970s American film[4]. This brief piece, no more than a few pages, which examined the new generation of American filmmakers, stuck out like a UFO in the landscape of institutional and mainstream film criticism of the time, but still made quite an impression on French cinephiles who'd been reading *Starfix* for a decade and nursing themselves on VHS tapes of '70s movies. From then on, established critics began reconsidering an entire range of often misunderstood movies. It was the start of a new theoretical approach, discreet and as yet invisible, that would lead ever more movie lovers to comment on the output of a relatively brief period in American film.

EVERY MOVEMENT IS ITS OWN MOMENT

But just what period are we talking about, exactly? One of the first difficulties in defining a moment—and here New Hollywood is no exception—is to determine when it began, and when it all came tumbling down. Historical movements often have several starting points—a whole string of them, which critic and historian Jean-Baptiste Thoret calls "matrices." To pick out a few of the most notable ones, he goes all the way back to 1954.

Giving New Hollywood a beginning and an ending isn't the best way to get critics on the same page. Some say it lasted from 1967 to 1983, others from 1965 to 1975; still others will swear it had all run out of gas as early as 1974... For the purposes of this nonfiction comic Jean-Baptiste Thoret has decided to frame New Hollywood between two significant and representative movies. He opens with that foundational film, Dennis Hopper's *Easy Rider*, and closes with Francis Ford Coppola's sepulchral *Apocalypse Now*, which, in terms of dates gives us 1969 to 1979. Of course, these dates are mere suggestions, since in his viewing list, Jean-Baptiste Thoret includes Frank Perry's *The Swimmer* (shot in 1966) and Arthur Penn's *Bonnie and Clyde* (released in 1967), not to mention Michael Cimino's *Heaven's Gate*, John Cassavetes' *Gloria* and Stanley Kubrick's *The Shining*, three movies that came out in 1980. For Thoret, New Hollywood's true death knell was sounded in the spring of 1981, with George Romero's *Knightriders*, an astonishing tale featuring Ed Harris as the "king" of a small traveling troupe of motorcycle "jousters," the "final expression of the late counterculture.[5]" *From Easy Rider to Knightriders* would've been just as good a title.

YOU KNOW, BILLY... WE BLEW IT.

And so it was, in the early aughts, that audiences, perusing the works of Peter Biskind in the U.S. and Jean-Baptiste Thoret in France, and the many books and articles that appeared in their wake—audiences already familiar with the films these works mentioned—could at last put a name to the constellation of directors representative of that period retroactively christened New Hollywood[6]. Each and every name in that constellation was charged with its own ideas and images. A list of the most famous included filmmakers as varied as Scorsese, Peckinpah, Cimino, Romero, Milius, Nichols, Siegel, Pakula, Coppola, Eastwood, Penn, Friedkin, Lucas, Polanski, Rafelson, Kubrick, Morrissey, Rosenberg, Sarafian, Hill, Yates, Schlesinger, Spielberg, Cassavetes, Winner, Allen, Forman, Ashby, Hopper, Altman, Schaffner, Fosse, Bogdanovich, Lumet, Brooks, Craven, De Palma, Pollack, Jewison, Boorman, Malick...

The cinematic output of these directors marked a break from the narrative conventions and production practices of Old Hollywood. This entire generation of filmmakers, but also actors and producers, positioned themselves against Old Hollywood. Against the old musicals, the old Westerns with their stately violence... Out with Freudian cinema, make way for readers of Wilhelm Reich and Timothy Leary[7]! This generation of mostly thirty year-olds was fascinated by the rise of French and Italian cinema, bathed in the counterculture, politicized, obsessed with American taboos against sex, corruption, violence, and injustices of social representation...

This new guard, however, not only made its mark on film itself, but also radically changed the way movies were made. This was an era when actors and directors seized power—"storming the Hollywood citadel," in Jean-Baptiste Thoret's well-chosen words.

Directors who wanted to become auteurs, actors who wanted to direct, a rejection of the great studio heads and their know-how, an appeal to outside financiers... The revolution was underway, inspired by the filmmakers of European New Waves and their appetite for life. With one crucial difference: unlike the Europeans, who'd created a certain independence for themselves from a system that they rejected, the American generation demanded artistic independence and studio infrastructure. A miracle happened, but as Jean-Baptiste Thoret explains in these pages, it was short-lived, and doomed to disaster right from the start. When they founded United Artists in 1919, Charlie Chaplin, Douglas Fairbanks, and Mary Pickford vowed to put artists at the center of the process. In the end, the New Hollywood generation had no more success than they did at changing the game; they may even have done more harm than anything else. "You know, Billy... We blew it."[8]

David Vandermeulen

NOTES

[1] Peter Biskind, *Easy Riders, Raging Bulls*: *How the Sex-Drugs-and-Rock-'n'-Roll generation saved Hollywood.* (Simon and Schuster, 1998). Published in France by Le Cherche midi, 2002. Since 2006, the French edition has been available in a paperback edition simply entitled *The New Hollywood.*

[2] Although most of these directors were born in the late 1930s, members of the famous New Hollywood generation weren't really all of the same generation. Their ranks included some who had been mobilized during World War II, like Franklin Schaffner (*Planet of the Apes, Papillon*), born in 1920; Arthur Penn (*Bonnie and Clyde, Little Big Man*), born in 1922; Sam Peckinpah (*Straw Dogs, The Getaway*), born in 1925; as well as the first baby boomers, like Steven Spielberg (*Sugarland Express, Jaws*), born in 1946.

[3] It would be unfair to say that no one at *Positif* or *Cahiers du Cinéma* appreciated New Hollywood. Some critics, like Olivier Assayas, Nicolas Saada, and Charles Tesson, had always shown their love for Carpenter, Friedkin, Craven, Siegel, Aldrich, Peckinpah, and Cimino, among others. However, their voices remained relatively fringe at the time, and did not represent the main editorial line of these monthlies with prestigious pasts.

[4] Jean-François Rauger, "Juste avant la nuit" ["Just Before the Night"] in *Cahiers du Cinéma n° 462*, pp.76-81, December 1992. Reprinted in the collection *L'oeil qui jouit* [*The Ecstatic Eye*], from Éditions Yellow Now in 2012.

[5] Jean-Baptiste Thoret, *Le Cinéma américain des années 70* [*American Cinema in the 1970s*], p.164 (*Cahiers du Cinéma*, 2006).

[6] When the first New Hollywood movies were coming out, American newspapers and magazines—*The New York Times, Newsweek, Time, The Village Voice*, almost exclusively NY-based, at first—used labels like the "American New Wave" or even "New Cinema," following the example of *Time* magazine's December 8, 1967 cover, which on the release of *Bonnie and Clyde* proclaimed: "New Cinema: Violence... Sex... Art..."

[7] Wilhelm Reich (1897-1957): Austrian doctor, psychiatrist, and sociologist of Jewish descent. This former pupil of Freud's went on to become one of his most famous naysayers, and contributed a great deal to sexology. He is primarily remembered for his commitment to emancipating the orgasm. Fleeing the Nazis, he emigrated to the U.S. and died of a heart attack in prison—that, at least, is the official story, since no autopsy was ever performed.

Timothy Leary (1920-1996): American neuropsychologist whose work extolled the therapeutic and spiritual benefits of LSD. His work was particularly influential on the hippie movement. Just like Reich, he was imprisoned multiple times.

[8] "At the end of Easy Rider, when Wyatt tells Billy 'We blew it,' he would be proved correct, although it would take over a decade to see it. Dennis Hopper and Peter Fonda had created an anthem for a generation, but they had also imagined its apocalyptic destruction." Peter Biskind, *Easy Riders, Raging Bulls*, 2008.

THE LITTLE BOOK
OF KNOWLEDGE:

NEW HOLLYWOOD

THERE WAS MADNESS IN ANY DIRECTION, AT ANY HOUR. IF NOT ACROSS THE BAY, THEN UP THE GOLDEN GATE OR DOWN 101 TO LOS ALTOS OR LA HONDA... YOU COULD STRIKE SPARKS ANYWHERE.

THERE WAS A FANTASTIC UNIVERSAL SENSE THAT WHATEVER WE WERE DOING WAS RIGHT, THAT WE WERE WINNING. AND THAT, I THINK, WAS THE HANDLE - THAT SENSE OF INEVITABLE VICTORY OVER THE FORCES OF OLD AND EVIL. NOT IN ANY MEAN OR MILITARY SENSE; WE DIDN'T NEED THAT.

OUR ENERGY WOULD SIMPLY PREVAIL. THERE WAS NO POINT IN FIGHTING - ON OUR SIDE OR THEIRS. WE HAD ALL THE MOMENTUM; WE WERE RIDING THE CREST OF A HIGH AND BEAUTIFUL WAVE.

SO NOW, LESS THAN FIVE YEARS LATER, YOU CAN GO UP ON A STEEP HILL IN LAS VEGAS AND LOOK WEST, AND WITH THE RIGHT KIND OF EYES YOU CAN ALMOST SEE THE HIGH-WATER MARK - THAT PLACE WHERE THE WAVE FINALLY BROKE AND ROLLED BACK.

HUNTER S. THOMPSON, *FEAR AND LOATHING IN LAS VEGAS*, 1971.

FROM THE LATE 1950S TO 1967, AMERICAN CINEMA ENTERED A DARK AGE, BESET BY DYING CLASSICISM, FALLING TICKET SALES, GROWING COMPETITION FROM TELEVISION, THE RISE OF DRIVE-INS, AND ABOVE ALL, THE EMERGENCE OF YOUNGER AUDIENCES WHO DEMANDED OTHER THINGS THAN WHAT THE STUDIOS KEPT PUTTING OUT. AND SO, UNSURE OF THEMSELVES, AMERICAN FILMMAKERS CAST ABOUT, BORROWING AT FIRST FROM THE ITALIAN AND FRENCH NEW WAVES (*MICKEY ONE*) AND PSYCHOANALYSIS (*THE LEFT HANDED GUN*).

AT THE TIME, STUDIOS WERE STILL HEADED BY SEPTUAGENARIANS WHO'D GOTTEN THEIR START IN THE SILENT ERA, MUCH LIKE JACK WARNER. IN RESPONSE TO THIS NEW STATE OF AFFAIRS, STUDIO HEADS EMBARKED ON EVER COSTLIER AND MORE GRANDIOSE PROJECTS, SWAN SONGS OF PHARAONIC SPLENDOR, WHICH THEY BELIEVED WOULD LURE AUDIENCES BACK INTO THEATRES.

BUT FROM *CLEOPATRA* (1963), WHICH ALMOST RUINED FOX, TO *BATTLE OF BRITAIN* (GUY HAMILTON, 1969), FROM *HELLO, DOLLY!* (GENE KELLY, 1969) TO ROBERT WISE'S *STAR!*—ALL THESE MOVIES FAILED SPECTACULARLY.

THE RADICAL CHANGES THAT CAME ABOUT RIGHT FROM THE START OF THE '60S, THE WIDENING GAP BETWEEN THE STUDIOS AND THEIR AUDIENCES, ALLOWED A NEW GENERATION—THE MOVIE BRATS—TO TAKE CONTROL.

THE WORLD THEN SEEMED TO BE DIVIDED INTO TWO CAMPS. ON ONE SIDE: MINORITY UPRISINGS, POLITICAL ASSASSINATIONS, THE VIETNAM WAR, AND THE DAILY FEAR OF BEING DRAFTED. ON THE OTHER: THE HIPPIE DREAM, ITS PARADE OF LIBERATING PROMISES AND THE ADVENT OF FLOWER POWER. OLD HOLLYWOOD VS. NEW, A HANDFUL OF KINGPINS CLINGING TO OLD PRODUCTION METHODS VS. AN EMERGING GENERATION OF FILMMAKERS, SCREENWRITERS, PRODUCERS, ACTORS...

... AND AUDIENCES, WHO ONLY HAD EYES FOR THE VALUES EXTOLLED BY THE COUNTERCULTURE AND ITS NEW GURUS: TIMOTHY LEARY, BOB DYLAN, DENNIS HOPPER... SEX, DRUGS, PROTEST, ROCK N'ROLL, AND THE UTOPIA OF COMMUNAL LIVING WERE THE KEYWORDS OF THE DAY.

1967: THE YEAR ARTHUR PENN AND WARREN BEATTY TEAMED UP TO SHOOT *BONNIE AND CLYDE*, THE MOVIE THAT WOULD SHAKE THE VERY FOUNDATIONS OF OLD HOLLYWOOD.

A FEW MONTHS LATER, PETER FONDA, DENNIS HOPPER, AND BERT SCHNEIDER WOULD DEAL IT A DEATH BLOW WITH *EASY RIDER.*

"NEW HOLLYWOOD" WAS BORN, AND FOR THE FIRST TIME IN THE HISTORY OF AMERICAN CINEMA, FILMMAKERS BECAME FULL-FLEDGED AUTEURS (THE EUROPEAN NEW WAVES WERE PIVOTAL SOURCES OF INSPIRATION FOR THEM, AND AS SUCH, IMPOSED THEIR RULES ON STUDIO HEADS.

IT WAS THE BEGINNING OF AN ENCHANTED INTERLUDE THAT LASTED THIRTEEN YEARS, FROM 1967 TO 1980. IT SAW A SPATE OF NEW NAMES—DIRECTORS, ACTORS, WRITERS, PRODUCERS—AND A FLOOD OF FILMS THAT REINVENTED AMERICAN CINEMA AND HAVE SINCE BECOME CLASSICS.

THE 1970S: THE LAST GOLDEN AGE OF AMERICAN CINEMA, AND THE GREAT ROMANTIC FRONTIER OF CONTEMPORARY FILM.

AT THE END OF *EASY RIDER*—THE MOVIE THAT, ALONG WITH *BONNIE AND CLYDE*, SHOT TWO YEARS EARLIER, KICKED OFF THE GOLDEN AGE OF AMERICAN CINEMA (1967-1980)—PETER FONDA REPEATS A LINE TO DENNIS HOPPER, A LINE IMPROVISED ON SET, THAT WAS TO BECOME EMBLEMATIC: "WE BLEW IT!" NEW HOLLYWOOD HAD NOT YET BEGUN, AND ALREADY, ONE OF ITS INSTIGATORS WAS (UNWITTINGLY?) PROPHESYING ITS DOWNFALL.

NEW HOLLYWOOD:
FROM *EASY RIDER* TO *APOCALYPSE NOW*

...THE YEAR OF THE CRACK-UP, IN THE FITZGERALDIAN SENSE OF THE WORD. THE TRUE BREAK WOULD COME IN 1967. BUT 1963 WAS THE YEAR OF *CLEOPATRA*, THE YEAR CERTAIN GREAT DIRECTORS IN THE HOLLYWOOD TRADITION MADE THEIR FINAL FILMS: JOHN FORD, WITH *THE MAN WHO SHOT LIBERTY VALANCE*, RAOUL WALSH (IN 1964) WITH *A DISTANT TRUMPET*.

DURING THIS TIME, EUROPEAN CINEMA WAS GOING THROUGH ITS OWN GOLDEN AGE AND REVOLUTION: WITH ANTONIONI, FELLINI, RISI, AND GERMI IN ITALY, BERGMAN IN SWEDEN, AND THE FRENCH NEW WAVE.

IT WAS ALSO THE YEAR *JFK* WAS *ASSASSINATED*, ON NOVEMBER 22—A MAJOR EVENT IN AMERICAN HISTORY, AND THE INDISPUTABLE MATRIX (VIA IMAGES AND THE ZAPRUDER FOOTAGE) FOR AMERICAN MOVIES TO COME.

ON THAT FATEFUL MORNING OF NOVEMBER 22, A MAN ARMED WITH A HIGH-END MODEL 414 PD BELL & HOWELL ZOOMATIC DIRECTOR SERIES CAMERA POSITIONED HIMSELF ATOP A CONCRETE PEDESTAL IN DALLAS' DEALEY PLAZA. GARMENT MANUFACTURER *ABRAHAM ZAPRUDER* HAD NOT IMAGINED THAT THE AMATEUR FOOTAGE HE WAS ABOUT TO EXPOSE, 26 SECONDS OF 8MM HOME MOVIE LIKE COUNTLESS OTHERS HE'D MADE, WOULD BECOME THE MOST PORED-OVER FILM IN THE HISTORY OF AMERICAN IMAGES, AND OF COURSE, AMERICAN CINEMA.

FROM JACKIE KENNEDY'S PINK SUIT TO THE REASON JFK'S HEAD EXPLODED (A MOMENT THE FILM'S ANALYSTS REFERRED TO AS "Z 313", AFTER THE FRAME NUMBER); FROM THE ASSASSINATION OF A POLITICAL LEADER IN A MOTORCADE TO THE PRESENCE OF AN UNSEEN SNIPER LYING IN WAIT; FROM THE EXISTENCE OF FILM-AS-EVIDENCE, SUPPOSEDLY CONTAINING THE TRUTH OF AN EVENT, TO THE CONVICTION OF WIDESPREAD CONSPIRACY, THE ZAPRUDER FOOTAGE AND ITS INNUMERABLE INTERPRETATIONS FORMED A MASSIVE BODY OF MOTIFS THAT HAS, IN WAYS BOTH AVOWED AND UNDERGROUND, INFLUENCED AMERICAN MOVIES FROM THE LATE 1960S TO TODAY.

THE LIST IS ENDLESS: *NASHVILLE, THE PARALLAX VIEW, THE CONVERSATION, BONNIE AND CLYDE,* MOST OF BRIAN DE PALMA'S OEUVRE (FROM *GREETINGS* TO *SNAKE EYES*), *THE DOMINO PRINCIPLE, THE SHOOTING,* CLINT EASTWOOD'S *A PERFECT WORLD,* ALL THE PARANOID MOVIES OF THE MID-'70S, THE ERA'S REALIST HORROR MOVIES, ALL THE WAY TO OLIVER STONE'S *JFK* IN 1992. JFK'S ASSASSINATION, AND THE FILM THAT OFFERED IT UP FOR ALL TO SEE, BECAME A GHOST THAT HAUNTED POST-1963 AMERICAN CINEMA.

MANY MOVIES, LIKE *THE PARALLAX VIEW, THE CONVERSATION,* AND *BLOW OUT,* OFFERED UP IMPASSIONED FICTIONAL REIMAGININGS OF THOSE "SEVEN SECONDS THAT BROKE THE BACK OF THE AMERICAN CENTURY." (DON DELILLO, *LIBRA*)

HOW DID AN AMATEUR FILM COME TO ALTER THE CODES FOR THE DEPICTION OF VIOLENCE AND MURDER IN AMERICAN MOVIES OF THE '60S AND '70S?

FOR JFK'S ASSASSINATION INTRODUCED DOUBT AND NECESSITATED A SYSTEMATIC CRITIQUE OF AMERICA'S REIGNING VALUES.

IN THE MIDDLE OF THE 1960S, WHEN AMERICAN CINEMA WAS SEARCHING FOR ITS OWN IDENTITY, CERTAIN FILMS WOULD ESTABLISH THEMSELVES AS CORNERSTONES OF THE REVOLUTION. *SHADOWS*, IN 1959; *IN COLD BLOOD, THE MANCHURIAN CANDIDATE...*

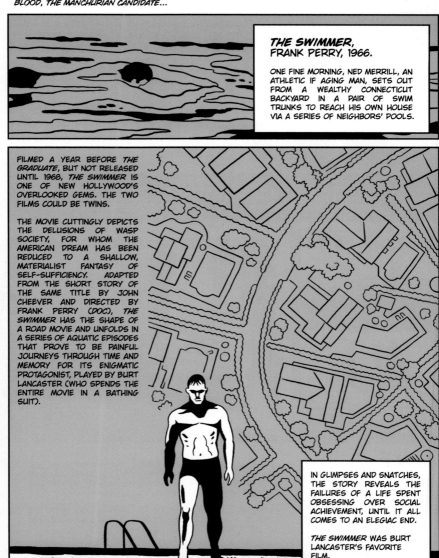

THE SWIMMER,
FRANK PERRY, 1966.

ONE FINE MORNING, NED MERRILL, AN ATHLETIC IF AGING MAN, SETS OUT FROM A WEALTHY CONNECTICUT BACKYARD IN A PAIR OF SWIM TRUNKS TO REACH HIS OWN HOUSE VIA A SERIES OF NEIGHBORS' POOLS.

FILMED A YEAR BEFORE *THE GRADUATE*, BUT NOT RELEASED UNTIL 1968, *THE SWIMMER* IS ONE OF NEW HOLLYWOOD'S OVERLOOKED GEMS. THE TWO FILMS COULD BE TWINS.

THE MOVIE CUTTINGLY DEPICTS THE DELUSIONS OF WASP SOCIETY, FOR WHOM THE AMERICAN DREAM HAS BEEN REDUCED TO A SHALLOW, MATERIALIST FANTASY OF SELF-SUFFICIENCY. ADAPTED FROM THE SHORT STORY OF THE SAME TITLE BY JOHN CHEEVER AND DIRECTED BY FRANK PERRY (DOC), *THE SWIMMER* HAS THE SHAPE OF A ROAD MOVIE AND UNFOLDS IN A SERIES OF AQUATIC EPISODES THAT PROVE TO BE PAINFUL JOURNEYS THROUGH TIME AND MEMORY FOR ITS ENIGMATIC PROTAGONIST, PLAYED BY BURT LANCASTER (WHO SPENDS THE ENTIRE MOVIE IN A BATHING SUIT).

IN GLIMPSES AND SNATCHES, THE STORY REVEALS THE FAILURES OF A LIFE SPENT OBSESSING OVER SOCIAL ACHIEVEMENT, UNTIL IT ALL COMES TO AN ELEGIAC END.

THE SWIMMER WAS BURT LANCASTER'S FAVORITE FILM.

SECONDS, JOHN FRANKENHEIMER, 1966.

OF ALL THE AMERICAN DIRECTORS WHO EMERGED IN THE LATE '50S AND EARLY '60S—ARTHUR PENN, SIDNEY LUMET, AND EVEN ROBERT ALTMAN—JOHN FRANKENHEIMER WAS, WITHOUT A DOUBT (ALONG WITH JOHN CASSAVETES) THE QUICKEST AND EARLIEST TO FORGE AN INCREDIBLY PERSONAL STYLE.

SECONDS, HIS EIGHTH FILM AND THE THIRD IN A PARANOID TRILOGY BEGUN IN 1962 WITH *THE MANCHURIAN CANDIDATE*, IS RADICAL AND DIZZYING EVIDENCE THEREOF.

SECONDS

SOMEWHERE BETWEEN ANTONIONI'S *L'ECLISSE*, THE VIOLENTLY AUTEURIST ACTS OF ORSON WELLES, AND *THE TWILIGHT ZONE*, *SECONDS* OFFERS A STRIKING SUMMATION OF THE MAN WHO, IN THE '60S AND '70S, WOULD BECOME THE GREAT AMERICAN FILMMAKER OF MODERN ALIENATION.

BONNIE AND CLYDE

They're young...they're in love...and they kill people.

1967.

THE BLOOD-SOAKED, TRAGIC EPIC OF CLYDE BARROW AND BONNE PARKER OFFENDED CONSERVATIVES AND STUDIO BIG SHOTS, BUT ARTHUR PENN'S FILM STRUCK A CHORD WITH YOUNG AUDIENCES.

IN THIS PERIOD OF ANTI-WAR DEMONSTRATIONS, GHETTO RIOTS (WATTS, 1965), FREE-FLOATING ANGER, AND GENERAL QUESTIONING OF THE AMERICAN WAY OF LIFE, *BONNIE AND CLYDE* AMOUNTED TO A MANIFESTO.

THE GENERATION OF THE SUMMER OF LOVE AND FLOWER POWER FINALLY SAW THEMSELVES IN A MOVIE: A MOVIE THAT REFLECTED THE ANTI-ESTABLISHMENT HUMOR OF THE TIMES.

IT'S REALLY A VERY ORDINARY STORY, WHAT HAPPENS TO THESE YOUNG PEOPLE. EXCEPT WE WERE ABLE TO TELL IT IN AN EXCITING NEW WAY.

WARNER HATED THE MOVIE, SO WARREN BEATTY TOOK OVER DISTRIBUTION AND SALES. MOST CRITICS HATED THE MOVIE TOO. THEN PAULINE KAEL WROTE A REVIEW SINGING ITS PRAISES AND SUDDENLY, THINGS BEGAN TO CHANGE.

PEOPLE THOUGHT THE FILM WAS VIOLENT, BUT BACK THEN, WE WERE SEEING PEOPLE GET KILLED IN VIETNAM ON THE NEWS EVERY NIGHT!

ARTHUR PENN

"ONLY A FEW YEARS AGO, A GOOD DIRECTOR WOULD HAVE SUGGESTED THE VIOLENCE OBLIQUELY, WITH REACTION SHOTS... DEATH MIGHT HAVE BEEN SYMBOLIZED BY A LIGHT GOING OUT, OR STYLIZED, WITH BLOOD AND WOUNDS KEPT TO A MINIMUM... BUT THE WHOLE POINT OF *BONNIE AND CLYDE* IS TO RUB OUR NOSES IN IT, TO MAKE US PAY OUR DUES FOR LAUGHING."

"THE DIRTY REALITY OF DEATH - NOT SUGGESTIONS BUT BLOOD AND HOLES - IS NECESSARY... I THINK THAT THIS TIME PENN IS RIGHT. *BONNIE AND CLYDE* NEEDS VIOLENCE; VIOLENCE IS ITS MEANING."

"*BONNIE AND CLYDE* BRINGS INTO THE ALMOST FRIGHTENINGLY PUBLIC WORLD OF MOVIES THINGS THAT PEOPLE HAVE BEEN FEELING AND SAYING AND WRITING ABOUT."

PAULINE KAEL, 1967.

MEANWHILE, PARAMOUNT WAS BOUGHT OUT BY CHARLES BLUHDORN, AN AUSTRIAN BUSINESSMAN WHO KNEW NOTHING ABOUT FILM. MOVIES WERE HIS PLAYTHING.

...MUSIC, SONGS, AND LAUGHTER, EVANS—NOW THAT'S WHAT AUDIENCES WANT!

MUSICALS? ARE YOU SURE, SIR?

ABSOLUTELY! HAVE TO GO NOW, GOT ANOTHER CALL.

ROBERT EVANS STARTED OUT BY GRANTING HIS BOSS'S ANACHRONISTIC WISHES, PRODUCING GLAMOROUS MUSICALS: *PAINT YOUR WAGON*, *DARLING LILI*... ALL FLOPS, WHICH AUDIENCES AVOIDED AND CRITICS EVISCERATED.

EVANS CHANGED TACK AND SOUGHT OUT ROMAN POLANSKI, A POLISH DIRECTOR WHOSE FILMS (*CUL-DE-SAC*, *REPULSION*, AND *THE FEARLESS VAMPIRE KILLERS*) HAD MADE QUITE AN IMPRESSION ON AMERICAN FANS.

THE RESULT WAS *ROSEMARY'S BABY*, ADAPTED FROM IRA LEVIN'S NOVEL OF THE SAME NAME AND PRODUCED BY THE HIGH PRIEST OF B-MOVIE HORROR, WILLIAM CASTLE.

A PINNACLE OF THE GENRE, *ROSEMARY'S BABY*, ALONG WITH ROMERO'S *NIGHT OF THE LIVING DEAD* THAT SAME YEAR, INAUGURATED THE MODERN ERA OF HORROR MOVIES.

GONE WERE THE DAYS WHEN THE THREAT CAME FROM MARS OR TRANSYLVANIA: FROM NOW ON, THE DEMON DWELLED AMONG US, IN THE VERY HEART OF AMERICA, IN THE WOMB OF A YOUNG NEW YORKER.

ROMAN POLANSKI:

"AS AN AGNOSTIC, I BELIEVED NEITHER IN SATAN AS THE INCARNATION OF EVIL, OR IN A PERSONAL GOD; SUCH IDEAS CONTRADICTED MY RATIONAL WORLD VIEW.

FOR CREDIBILITY'S SAKE, I DECIDED THAT THERE WOULD HAVE TO BE A LOOPHOLE: THE POSSIBILITY THAT ROSEMARY'S SUPERNATURAL EXPERIENCES WERE FIGMENTS OF HER IMAGINATION.

THE ENTIRE STORY, AS SEEN THROUGH HER EYES COULD HAVE BEEN A CHAIN OF ONLY SUPERFICIALLY SINISTER COINCIDENCES, A PRODUCT OF HER FEVERISH FANCIES. THAT IS WHY A THREAD OF DELIBERATE AMBIGUITY RUNS THROUGHOUT THE FILM."

MIA FARROW, WHO WAS MARRIED TO FRANK SINATRA AT THE TIME, WAS CAST IN THE ROLE OF ROSEMARY, AND JOHN CASSAVETES AS HER HUSBAND AFTER WARREN BEATTY TURNED DOWN THE ROLE.

AFTER THIS MASTERPIECE, A HORRIFIC TRAGEDY TOOK PLACE: IN AUGUST 1969, THE MANSON FAMILY MURDERED POLANSKI'S WIFE SHARON TATE IN BEVERLY HILLS.

IN 1971, POLANSKI RETURNED TO FILMMAKING WITH A BLOOD-SPATTERED VERSION OF SHAKESPEARE'S *MACBETH*, THEN TACKLED ANOTHER GENRE: FILM NOIR.

THE RESULT: *CHINATOWN*, WITH FAYE DUNAWAY AND JACK NICHOLSON.

THIS DARK, IRONIC MOVIE FIT IN PERFECTLY WITH THE ERA'S CONSPIRACY FILMS, CONVEYING POST-WATERGATE SUSPICION OF ALL INSTITUTIONS.

ROGER CORMAN

SINCE THE LATE 1950S, ROGER CORMAN HAD REIGNED OVER A STABLE OF YOUNG FILMMAKERS, MOST OF WHOM WOULD GO ON TO BE MAJOR PLAYERS IN THE NEW HOLLYWOOD: MARTIN SCORSESE, PETER BOGDANOVICH, PETER FONDA, FRANCIS FORD COPPOLA, MONTE HELLMAN, JOE DANTE, ETC.

CORMAN'S FILMS WERE EXPLOITATION FLICKS, SHOT ON A SHOESTRING IN UNDER A WEEK, CATERING TO THE EXPECTATIONS OF YOUNG AUDIENCES STUDIOS DIDN'T KNOW EXISTED. HIS MOVIES, RIPPED FROM THE HEADLINES AND HIP TO CHANGING LIFESTYLES (MOTORCYCLES, LSD, GANGS, ETC.), WERE SHOWN IN 5000 DRIVE-INS ACROSS THE LAND.

AFTER A SERIES DEVOTED TO EDGAR ALLAN POE ADAPTATIONS, CORMAN PRODUCED *THE WILD ANGELS* WITH PETER FONDA IN 1966, AND THEN *THE ST. VALENTINE'S DAY MASSACRE* AND *THE TRIP* THE NEXT YEAR.

28

JOE DANTE: WHEN YOU WERE STARTING OUT WITH ROGER CORMAN, YOU DIDN'T THINK OF YOURSELF AS PART OF THE MOVIE INDUSTRY, YOU WERE PART OF THE CORMAN INDUSTRY, BECAUSE CORMAN FILMS AND NEW WORLD PICTURES HAD SUCH LIMITED DISTRIBUTION, ON THE FRINGES OF THE MAJOR NETWORKS, AND WEREN'T COVERED BY CRITICS OR SO-CALLED "SERIOUS" MAGAZINES.

ONLY LATER, ONCE I'D WORKED FOR THE STUDIOS, WAS I THOUGHT OF AS A STUDIO DIRECTOR. BUT I STILL FELT LIKE A "CORMAN DIRECTOR," A DIRECTOR OF B-MOVIES.

BUT LITTLE BY LITTLE, B-MOVIES BECAME A-MOVIES IN HOLLYWOOD. AND TODAY, HOLLYWOOD PRODUCES VERY EXPENSIVE SUPERHERO MOVIES, BLOCKBUSTERS ADAPTED FROM COMIC BOOKS, ETC., WHEREAS THIRTY YEARS AGO ALL THAT STUFF—THE WORLD OF COMICS, SUPERHEROES, GIANT MONSTERS—BELONGED TO B-MOVIES!

NOW, FILMMAKERS OF MY GENERATION, WHO GREW UP ON THESE LITTLE MOVIES, ON POP AND UNDERGROUND CULTURE, BENEFITED FROM THIS TRANSFORMATION IN HOLLYWOOD, WHEN THIS STUFF WENT MAINSTREAM. BUT I'D HAVE BEEN PERFECTLY HAPPY JUST PLUGGING AWAY, MAKING B-MOVIES ON SHOESTRING BUDGETS FOR THE REST OF MY LIFE.

IN THE MID-1960S, FORMER FILM CRITIC PETER BOGDANOVICH MET ROGER CORMAN, WHO OFFERED TO LET HIM HEAD A SECOND UNIT ON *THE WILD ANGELS*.

IN RETURN, CORMAN AGREED TO PRODUCE BOGDANOVICH'S FIRST MOVIE, *TARGETS*, IN 1967.

ON ONE CONDITION: THAT HE USE BORIS KARLOFF, WHO STILL OWED CORMAN TWO DAYS OF WORK. AND—WHY NOT?—CLIPS FROM *THE TERROR*, A GOTHIC HORROR MOVIE SHOT WITH KARLOFF AND JACK NICHOLSON IN 1963.

TARGETS:
ON THE EVE OF RETIREMENT, AN AGING HORROR STAR (PLAYED BY BORIS KARLOFF) AGREES TO INTRODUCE HIS FINAL FILM AT ITS PREMIERE.

MEANWHILE, A YOUNG AMERICAN COLDLY SLAUGHTERS HIS FAMILY BEFORE RANDOMLY KILLING AS MANY PEOPLE AS HE CAN. THE TWO MEN FACE OFF AT THE DRIVE-IN HOSTING THE PREMIERE.

ONE OF THE FILM'S SOURCES: ON AUGUST 1, 1966, CHARLES WHITMAN CLIMBED ATOP THE TEXAS TOWER AT THE UNIVERSITY OF TEXAS AUSTIN AND OPENED FIRE ON THE CROWD BELOW. SIXTEEN PEOPLE DIED. HE WAS SHOT DOWN BY THE POLICE AFTER A SIEGE LASTING SEVERAL HOURS.

WITH ONE FOOT IN THE '70S AND ITS BOLD, FORMAL INNOVATIONS, AND THE OTHER PLANTED ADMIRINGLY IN THE GOLDEN AGE HOLLYWOOD OF JOHN FORD AND HOWARD HAWKS, WHOSE SURVIVAL HE WISHED TO ENSURE, BOGDANOVICH PURSUED A PATH THAT WAS, SHALL WE SAY, ELEGIAC, SEEKING A COMPROMISE BETWEEN CLASSICAL FORMS AND A FRESHNESS, EVEN CRUDENESS, INHERITED FROM EUROPEAN NEW WAVES AND LATE 1950S CASSAVETES.

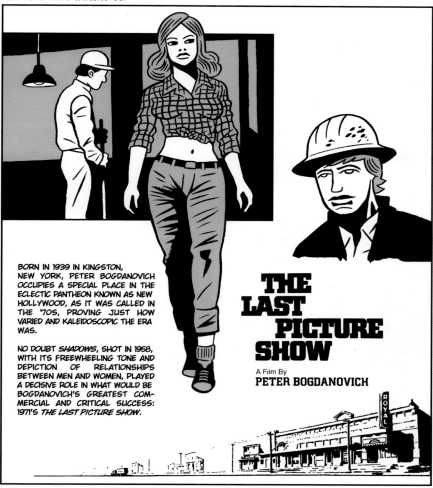

BORN IN 1939 IN KINGSTON, NEW YORK, PETER BOGDANOVICH OCCUPIES A SPECIAL PLACE IN THE ECLECTIC PANTHEON KNOWN AS NEW HOLLYWOOD, AS IT WAS CALLED IN THE '70S, PROVING JUST HOW VARIED AND KALEIDOSCOPIC THE ERA WAS.

NO DOUBT *SHADOWS*, SHOT IN 1958, WITH ITS FREEWHEELING TONE AND DEPICTION OF RELATIONSHIPS BETWEEN MEN AND WOMEN, PLAYED A DECISIVE ROLE IN WHAT WOULD BE BOGDANOVICH'S GREATEST COMMERCIAL AND CRITICAL SUCCESS: 1971'S *THE LAST PICTURE SHOW*.

THE LAST PICTURE SHOW

A Film By
PETER BOGDANOVICH

BOGDANOVICH PLANTED HIS CAMERA IN A SLEEPY TOWN DEEP IN THE HEART OF TEXAS AND, ON ORSON WELLES' ADVICE, SHOT IN BLACK AND WHITE, SURROUNDING HIMSELF WITH A GENERATION OF YOUNG, PROMISING ACTORS—JEFF BRIDGES, CYBIL SHEPHERD, TIMOTHY BOTTOMS, ELLEN BURSTYN—AS WELL AS BEN JOHNSON, ONE OF JOHN FORD'S REGULARS.

PRODUCED BY BBS, THE SMALL BUT BUSY PRODUCTION COMPANY THAT HAD JUST PUT OUT *EASY RIDER* AND *FIVE EASY PIECES*, *THE LAST PICTURE SHOW* MADE BOGDANOVICH'S NAME AS THE NEW WUNDERKIND OF THE EARLY '70S.

YOU KNOW... THIS USED TO BE A HELL OF A GOOD COUNTRY. I CAN'T UNDERSTAND WHAT'S GONE WRONG WITH IT.

EVERYBODY GOT CHICKEN, THAT'S WHAT... THEY THINK WE'D CUT THEIR THROAT. THEY'RE SCARED.

THEY'RE NOT SCARED OF YOU. THEY'RE SCARED OF WHAT YOU REPRESENT TO THEM.

OH, NO. WHAT YOU REPRESENT TO THEM... IS FREEDOM.

ALL WE REPRESENT TO THEM IS SOMEBODY WHO NEEDS A HAIRCUT.

FREEDOM'S WHAT IT'S ALL ABOUT.

OH YEAH, THAT'S RIGHT. THAT'S WHAT IT'S ALL ABOUT. BUT TALKING ABOUT IT AND BEING IT... THAT'S TWO DIFFERENT THINGS. IT'S REAL HARD TO BE FREE WHEN YOU ARE BOUGHT AND SOLD IN THE MARKETPLACE.

DON'T TELL ANYBODY THAT THEY'RE NOT FREE, BECAUSE THEY'LL GET BUSY KILLING AND MAIMING... TO PROVE TO YOU THAT THEY ARE.

THEY'RE GOING TO TALK TO YOU AND TALK TO YOU... ABOUT INDIVIDUAL FREEDOM. BUT THEY SEE A FREE INDIVIDUAL, IT'S GOING TO SCARE THEM.

WELL, IT DON'T MAKE THEM RUNNING SCARED.

IT MAKES THEM DANGEROUS.

DIRECTOR DENNIS HOPPER'S FIRST FILM RESEMBLED A WESTERN GONE WRONG. TAKING UP THE PIONEERS' JOURNEY, BUT IN THE OTHER DIRECTION, AND TOWARD NOTHINGNESS (DEATH), UNDER THE INFLUENCE OF "BEAT" MANIFESTOS BY JACK KEROUAC (*ON THE ROAD*) AND ITS PROTAGONIST DUO, THE MEDITATIVE SAL PARADISE AND THE OBSESSIVE DEAN MORIARTY (A.K.A. NEAL CASSADY).

HOPPER: "OUR TWO CHARACTERS ARE ACTUALLY COWBOYS; THEY COULD JUST AS WELL'VE BEEN RIDING HORSES INSTEAD OF MOTORCYCLES. THEY'RE LIKE GUNSLINGERS WHO RIDE INTO TOWN, AND THE TOWNSPEOPLE TRY TO RUN THEM OUT AS FAST AS THEY CAN. THEY GET ALONG WITH HIPPIES, WHO'RE LIKE INDIANS IN OLD WESTERNS."

HOW COULD THE NEW HOLLYWOOD (AND EVERYONE WHO DREAMED OF BREAKING THE RULES: COPPOLA, SCORSESE, AND US) REALLY WORK? THE ESTABLISHMENT HATED THEM ALL SO MUCH, Y'KNOW.... BUT SINCE THEIR MOVIES WERE HITS, STUDIOS HAD TO BACK THEM.

TO THEM, WE WERE A NIGHTMARE. THAT'S WHY, AS SOON AS THEY COULD TAKE BACK CONTROL, THEY DIDN'T HESITATE FOR A SECOND!

PETER FONDA

AT FIRST, THEY DIDN'T BELIEVE THAT REBELLIOUS YOUNG PEOPLE WERE AN AUDIENCE, THAT HIPPIES WERE AN AUDIENCE. THEY DIDN'T FIGURE THAT OUT TILL 1968, JUST AS WE WERE SHOOTING *EASY RIDER*, WHEN YOUNG PEOPLE ALL OVER THE WORLD, FROM PARIS TO SAN FRANCISCO, WERE HUNGRY FOR CHANGE AND ROSE UP EVERYWHERE AGAINST AUTHORITY.

AFTER THE KENT STATE SHOOTINGS, NEIL YOUNG WROTE "OHIO" WHEN HE SAW THE PHOTOS IN *LIFE* MAGAZINE. "OHIO" BECAME A HYMN FOR OUR GENERATION...

"TIN SOLDIERS AND NIXON COMING, WE'RE FINALLY ON OUR OWN. THIS SUMMER I HEAR THE DRUMMING, FOUR DEAD IN OHIO."

THAT WAS THE EXACT FEELING WE WANTED TO GET ACROSS IN *EASY RIDER*, AND ALSO WITH ITS SOUNDTRACK: HOPELESSNESS. WE WERE SO ON EDGE THAT WE DIDN'T WANT PEOPLE WHO SAW THE FILM THINKING THERE WAS ANY HOPE IF WE KEPT LETTING THE ESTABLISHMENT ACT THE WAY IT DID.

WE WANTED PEOPLE TO THINK ABOUT EVERYTHING THE FILM DEPICTED: RACISM, BIGOTRY, PURITANISM, STUPIDITY, INTOLERANCE, IGNORANCE... BUT INSTEAD OF JUST SAYING IT WITH WORDS, WE HAD TO SHOW IT.

EASY RIDER WAS PRODUCED BY BBS, A SMALL INDEPENDENT PRODUCTION COMPANY CO-FOUNDED IN 1965 BY PRODUCERS BERT SCHNEIDER AND BOB RAFELSON, WHO WENT ON TO REVOLUTIONIZE THE HISTORY OF AMERICAN FILM AND WERE THERE AT THE BEGINNING OF WHAT NO ONE BACK THEN WAS CALLING NEW HOLLYWOOD YET.

JEAN-BAPTISTE THORET

AT THE TIME, AND FOR A SHORT WHILE LATER, BBS WAS GROUND ZERO FOR TURNED-ON, TUNED-IN FILMMAKERS, A CROSSROADS OF THE AMERICAN CINEMATIC RENAISSANCE, WHERE YOU COULD RUN INTO PETER BOGDANOVICH, HENRY JAGLOM, DENNIS HOPPER, OR JACK NICHOLSON.

ITS FILMS EMBODIED THE TREND THAT CULMINATED IN THE EARLY '70S, MOVIES THAT EVINCED DISSATISFACTION, EVEN LONGSTANDING DOUBT WITH REGARD TO SOCIAL AND POLITICAL INSTITUTIONS, MOVIES THAT FEATURED CHARACTERS SUFFERING EXISTENTIAL ANGST, FRINGE ELEMENTS AND MALADJUSTED TYPES GOING IN CIRCLES, ADRIFT IN THE EMPTINESS AT THE HEART OF DAY-TO-DAY NORMAL AMERICA.

PETER BOGDANOVICH'S THE LAST PICTURE SHOW, PETER DAVIS' HEARTS AND MINDS, HENRY JAGLOM'S TRACKS, AND TERRENCE MALICK'S DAYS OF HEAVEN WERE AMONG ITS GREATEST HITS.

OH, I ALMOST FORGOT: IN 1968, WHILE COLUMBIA WAS GETTING READY TO RELEASE EASY RIDER IN JULY 1969, JEROME HELLMAN, A PRODUCER AT UNITED ARTISTS, PAID A VISIT TO A YOUNG BRITISH FILMMAKER, JOHN SCHLESINGER (FRESH OFF THE SUCCESS OF DARLING) AND ASKED HIM WHAT HE WANTED TO DO NEXT.

THE RESULT? MIDNIGHT COWBOY, WITH JOHN VOIGT AND DUSTIN HOFFMAN. THE FIRST STUDIO FILM TO GET AN X RATING.

35

1969: *THE WILD BUNCH*, THE *CITIZEN KANE* OF NEW HOLLYWOOD

IN AMERICAN CINEMA OF THE 1970S, THERE WAS A BEFORE AND AN AFTER.

IF *EASY RIDER* HAD INDISPUTABLY SET THE NEW HOLLYWOOD MACHINE IN MOTION, IT WAS *THE WILD BUNCH* THAT, FROM AN AESTHETIC AND FORMAL POINT OF VIEW, PAVED THE WAY FOR THE FINAL GOLDEN AGE OF AMERICAN FILM.

IF THE FINAL SHOOTOUT IN *BONNIE AND CLYDE* OPENED A CONVERSATION ABOUT THE PROPER DEPICTION OF VIOLENCE, THEN WITH THE BLOOD-SOAKED FINALE TO *THE WILD BUNCH*— ITS OVER-THE-TOP GRATUITOUSNESS, ITS GRAPHIC EXCESS, ITS DISREGARD FOR CLASSICAL RULES OF POINT-OF-VIEW—THE CONVERSATION BECAME A FULL-FLEDGED DEBATE, ONE THAT RAGES ON TODAY OVER OTHER DIRECTORS (DE PALMA, WOO, TARANTINO, STONE, AND VERHOEVEN, TO NAME BUT A FEW). THE SURPRISING THING IS HOW LITTLE THE TERMS OF THE DEBATE HAVE CHANGED.

IN THE FILMS OF SAM PECKINPAH—NICKNAMED "BLOODY SAM"—VIOLENCE COMES ON LIKE A STORM, A DEVASTATING HURRICANE SWEEPING EVERYTHING UP IN ITS WAKE: MEN, OBJECTS, CAMERA ANGLES. THE DIRECTOR OF *THE WILD BUNCH* SHOT VIOLENCE FOR ITS OWN SAKE, FROM THE POV OF ITS OWN ENERGY, THE ATMOSPHERE IT IMPOSED, RATHER THAN THE INDIVIDUAL OR GROUP ACTION THAT LEGITIMIZED IT.

AS A RESULT, KNOWING WHO WAS FIRING OR FALLING, WHO WAS RIGHT OR WRONG, NO LONGER MATTERED AT ALL. THE FILM PUT ITSELF RIGHT IN THE MIDDLE OF THE VIOLENCE, WHICH IT ENVISIONED AS A PURE DISRUPTIVE FORCE, INDEPENDENT OF THE CHARACTERS AND THEIR RESPECTIVE ACTIONS.

UNTIL THEN, HOLLYWOOD CINEMA HAD FILMED NOT VIOLENCE BUT VIOLENT INDIVIDUALS. THIS WAS KNOWN AS THE SYSTEM OF THE "ACTION-IMAGE," A SYSTEM IN WHICH VIOLENCE WAS ATTACHED TO SPECIFIC INDIVIDUALS AS A MEANS TO SPECIFIC ENDS.

WITH SAM PECKINPAH, AMERICAN CINEMA TOOK A TURN TOWARD THE "ENERGY-IMAGE," FINALLY ACKNOWLEDGING ITS OWN ESSENTIAL NATURE. THE DISTINCTION BETWEEN "GOOD" AND "BAD" VIOLENCE COLLAPSED, GIVING WAY TO UNMOTIVATED, UNCONTROLLABLE, ONTOLOGICAL VIOLENCE, FREED AT LAST OF THE IDEOLOGY OF CLASSICAL HOLLYWOOD CINEMA, WHICH HAD LEGITIMIZED IT.

ROBERT ALTMAN

BORN IN 1925 IN MISSOURI AND TRAINED IN TELEVISION, ALTMAN MADE HIS HOLLYWOOD DEBUT IN 1967. HIS CAREER KICKED OFF IN 1970 WITH *M.A.S.H.* AFTER MAKING THE ROUNDS OF MANY DIRECTORS WHO ALL TURNED IT DOWN, RING LARDNER JR.'S SCREENPLAY ENDED UP IN ALTMAN'S HANDS. ALTMAN REWORKED THE STORY, BREATHED HIPPIE LIFE INTO IT, AND EXPANDED THE SATIRICAL ASPECT.

M.A.S.H. PORTRAYED THE DISSOLUTE, BURLESQUE LIFE IN A MILITARY HOSPITAL DURING THE KOREAN WAR WHICH, IN 1970, WAS NATURALLY TAKING PLACE IN VIETNAM. THE FILM BECAME ONE OF THE STANDARDS OF NEW HOLLYWOOD IN ITS BLANKET DISRESPECT FOR THE FOUNDING VALUES OF THE UNITED STATES.

IMMEDIATELY UPON RELEASE, IT BECAME A HUGE HIT AND RECEIVED THE PALME D'OR AT THE 1970 CANNES FILM FESTIVAL.

WARNER BROS. OFFERED ALTMAN A WESTERN. THE RESULT: *MCCABE & MRS. MILLER*, AN ARCHETYPAL ANTI-WESTERN WITH WARREN BEATTY AND JULIE CHRISTIE. THE PRODUCERS DISAPPROVED OF ALTMAN'S TREATMENT, BUT AUDIENCES WERE WON OVER. HE WAS NOW ONE OF THE MOST SOUGHT-AFTER DIRECTOR-PRODUCERS IN HOLLYWOOD.

IN 1973, HE DECIDED TO BRING A RAYMOND CHANDLER NOVEL (*THE LONG GOODBYE*) TO THE SCREEN, TEAMING UP ONCE MORE WITH ELLIOTT GOULD, TO WHOM HE GAVE THE ROLE OF PHILIP MARLOWE. ONCE AGAIN, ALTMAN DELIVERED A FILM OUT OF STEP WITH ITS GENRE, A NOIR WITH A PRIVATE EYE WHO TALKED TO HIMSELF AND ASKED EXISTENTIAL QUESTIONS ABOUT CANS OF CAT FOOD.

MCCABE & MRS. MILLER, 1971

THE OPENING CREDITS GIVE US A MAN WITH A FUNNY-LOOKING HAT MAKING HIS WAY SLOWLY ALONG UNDER GRAY AND RAINY SKIES, TO LEONARD COHEN'S MELANCHOLY SONG "THE STRANGER." IT WAS AN INVERSION OF CLASSIC WESTERN TROPES, WHICH TENDED TO SHOW SUNNY SKIES, WIDE OPEN SPACES, AND STRANGERS COMING TO TOWN. THAT SAID, WE ARE REMINDED OF SERGIO CORBUCCI'S *THE GREAT SILENCE*, AS IF AMERICAN FILM WERE ENGAGED IN THE SAME WORK OF DECONSTRUCTION AND "TRIVIALIZATION" THAT ITALIAN CINEMA HAD BEGUN IN THE MID-1960S.

THE FINAL SEQUENCE—THE FACE-OFF BETWEEN MCCABE AND THE THREE GUNMEN COME TO KILL HIM—IS THE OPPOSITE OF A CLASSICAL GENRE ENDING. FIRST OF ALL, ALTMAN CROSSCUTS BETWEEN TWO SEQUENCES: THE STANDOFF IN THE SNOW, AND THE BURNING OF THE LITTLE CHURCH IN TOWN. THESE TWO SEQUENCES INTERFERE WITH EACH OTHER AND WIND UP CANCELING EACH OTHER OUT, AS IF ALTMAN WERE RESISTING ANY MOMENTUM TOWARD A CLIMAX, THAT APEX OF THE CLASSICAL WESTERN WHEREIN THE PROTAGONIST CONFRONTS THE BAD GUYS WHILE THE TOWNSPEOPLE LOOK ON. HERE, MCCABE IS ALONE, THE TOWNSPEOPLE ARE BUSY WITH OTHER THINGS, SNOW FILLS THE FRAME SO COMPLETELY AS TO MAKE EVERYTHING A BLUR, AND MCCABE WINDS UP DYING, TO GENERAL INDIFFERENCE.

IN THE FINAL SHOT OF *MCCABE & MRS. MILLER*, A SODDEN, MELANCHOLY WESTERN THAT UNFOLDS TO LEONARD COHEN'S PLAINTIVE SONGS, JULIE CHRISTIE, THE MADAM OF A BROTHEL COVETED BY INIQUITOUS BRUTES, RETREATS FROM REALITY INTO CLOUDS OF OPIUM SMOKE.

ROBERT ALTMAN'S OEUVRE CAN BE SUMMED UP IN THIS IMAGE OF WITHDRAWAL, AS IF THERE WERE BUT TWO WAYS OF LIVING IN AMERICA AND THE WORLD: WITH ONE FOOT IN IT, CAVALIER AND NONCHALANT (AFTER ALL, ALL THE WORLD'S A STAGE), OR BOTH FEET OUT OF IT ALTOGETHER (THE SUICIDE OF THE WRITER PORTRAYED BY STERLING HAYDEN IN *THE LONG GOODBYE*).

FIVE EASY PIECES
(BOB RAFELSON, 1970)

FIVE EASY PIECES TRACES THE INDECISION OF BOBBY DUPEA, THE SON OF A MIDDLE-CLASS FAMILY OF MUSICIANS, PLAYED BY JACK NICHOLSON. AFTER HIS EYE-CATCHING CAMEO IN *EASY RIDER*, THIS WAS HIS FIRST MAJOR ROLE.

BOBBY WANDERS AROUND, DRIFTING FROM JOB TO JOB, BEFORE SETTLING DOWN AS AN OIL WORKER IN SOUTHERN CALIFORNIA, WHERE HE LIVES WITH RAYETTE (KAREN BLACK), A WAITRESS AT A BAR.

BOBBY DUPEA IS A TYPICAL MEMBER OF THAT FAMILY OF CHARACTERS WHO AREN'T AT HOME ANYWHERE IN 1960S AMERICA, LIKE THE TITULAR "GRADUATE" PLAYED BY DUSTIN HOFFMAN IN THE 1967 MIKE NICHOLS' FILM OF THE SAME NAME. BOBBY IS CHRONICALLY DISSATISFIED, UNCOMFORTABLE WHEREVER HE GOES, BE IT AMONG THE WORKING OR THE MIDDLE CLASSES. HE FEELS STIFLED AND IS ALWAYS TRYING TO ESCAPE HIS SURROUNDINGS. THIS NEED TO KEEP MOVING AMOUNTS TO A CURSE SINCE, DEEP DOWN, *HERE* NEVER WORKS OUT BUT *SOMEWHERE ELSE* NEVER LEADS ANYWHERE EITHER.

THE FILM MOCKS ALL THE TRADITIONAL MILIEUS: THE BLUE-COLLAR WORLD, THE UPPER CRUST, AND EVEN THE COUNTERCULTURE. THE LAST ESPECIALLY IN A HITCHHIKING SCENE WHERE TWO NARROW-MINDED FEMINIST ENVIRONMENTALISTS SPOUT CLICHÉS OF HIPPIE IDEOLOGY, ADVOCATING A RETURN TO NATURE—IN ALASKA, BECAUSE IT'S "WHITER," ONE OF THEM SAYS. THE FILM ESTABLISHES ITS DISTANCE FROM THE ILLUSIONS OF COMMUNAL LIVING VAUNTED IN *EASY RIDER*.

HAL ASHBY. WITH HIS UTTERLY UNIQUE WAY OF MIXING SATIRE AND DISENCHANTMENT, ASHBY IS ONE OF NEW HOLLYWOOD'S MAJOR VOICES. IN HIS DAY, ASHBY WAS THE EQUAL OF COPPOLA, FRIEDKIN, OR ROBERT ALTMAN, AND HAS SINCE PROVED A KEY INFLUENCE ON A GOOD NUMBER OF CONTEMPORARY AMERICAN FILMMAKERS AS WELL, STARTING WITH WES ANDERSON.

BORN IN 1929 TO A MORMON FAMILY, HAL ASHBY LEFT HIS NATIVE UTAH IN THE EARLY '50S, HEADING FOR CALIFORNIA AND THEN HOLLYWOOD, WHERE HE WORKED ODD JOBS BEFORE BECOMING AN EDITOR FOR NORMAN JEWISON, WHO WOULD BE HIS TRUE MENTOR.

IN 1970, HE DIRECTED *THE LANDLORD*, IN WHICH THE NAÏVE SON OF A NICE WHITE FAMILY COMES TO ACQUIRE A SMALL APARTMENT BUILDING IN THE BRONX WHOSE TENANTS ARE ALL BLACK. THE YEAR AFTER THAT, ASHBY DIRECTED ONE OF HIS MOST FAMOUS FILMS, *HAROLD AND MAUDE.*

OH, DINNER AT EIGHT, HAROLD.

ALL HAROLD (BUD CORT) WANTS TO DO IS DIE, OR RATHER TO STAGE HIS OWN SUICIDE SO THAT HIS MOTHER, A SHALLOW COMPOSITE OF NIXONIAN AMERICA, WILL DEIGN TO TAKE AN INTEREST IN HIM APART FROM GIVING HIM GLEAMING JAGUARS, WHICH HE IMMEDIATELY TURNS INTO HEARSES. HAROLD FEELS ALONE AND MISUNDERSTOOD UNTIL THE DAY WHEN THE WHIMSICAL, LIBERATING SPIRIT OF THE '60S COMES A-KNOCKING IN THE FORM OF MAUDE (RUTH GORDON), AN ECCENTRIC SEPTUAGENARIAN.

JUST LIKE THE NAÏVE GARDENER IN *BEING THERE* (PETER SELLERS), OR THE GUILELESS HAIRDRESSER IN *SHAMPOO* (WARREN BEATTY), HAROLD EMBODIES A KIND OF PURE INNOCENCE YET TO CONFRONT THE HARSH ORDEALS OF REALITY (FINDING A JOB, ENLISTING IN THE ARMY, GETTING MARRIED, ETC) HERE, AGAINST ALL EXPECTATIONS, THE VALUES OF THE '60S ARE TOUTED NOT BY YOUNG, FASHIONABLE ACTORS BUT A SPRUCE GRANDMA WHOM WE LEARN IN A RIVETING INSERT SHOT–A NUMBER TATTOOED ON HER ARM, WHICH LENDS THE STORY UNEXPECTED HEFT–IS A SURVIVOR OF THE NAZI CONCENTRATION CAMPS.

ASHBY DIED IN 1988, NO DOUBT A BIT TOO EARLY FOR THE WHOLESALE AUTEURIZATION, WHICH MOST NEW HOLLYWOOD FILMMAKERS ENJOYED, TO ELEVATE HIS FILMS TO THEIR RIGHTFUL PLACE IN THE HISTORY OF AMERICAN CINEMA.

THE FRIEDKIN CASE: WALKING THE LINE

IN THE 1970s, WILLIAM FRIEDKIN WAS COPPOLA'S ONLY SERIOUS RIVAL—HIS EVIL TWIN, IN A WAY: JUST AS MEGALOMANIACAL, JUST AS CRAZY. WITNESS *THE FRENCH CONNECTION*, *THE EXORCIST*, *CRUISING*, *TO LIVE AND DIE IN L.A.* AND EVEN HIS MASTERPIECE *SORCERER*, HIS MYSTICAL REMAKE OF CLOUZOT'S *THE WAGES OF FEAR*.

ALTHOUGH OFTEN IDENTIFIED WITH 1970s AMERICAN FILM (*CRISIS OF ACTION*, *UNCERTAIN STAKES*, *MORAL EQUIVALENCY*, ETC.), FRIEDKIN NEVERTHELESS OCCUPIED A FAIRLY FRINGE POSITION IN NEW HOLLYWOOD. LONG CONSIDERED A RIGHT-WING FILMMAKER WITH FASCIST TENDENCIES, UNAFRAID TO INVOKE THE DEVIL IN AN ERA MORE CONCERNED WITH THREATS CLOSER TO HOME, OR TO PLUCK SHAMELESSLY AT THE HEARTSTRINGS OF PERSONAL JUSTICE (*THE FRENCH CONNECTION*, AN EARLY DRAFT OF THE PRO-DEATH PENALTY ARGUMENT TO BE REFINED IN *RAMPAGE*), FRIEDKIN IS SOMETHING OF AN IDEOLOGICAL ANOMALY IN A MOVEMENT THAT IS BY AND LARGE CRITICAL OF THE AMERICAN WAY OF LIFE: ITS INSTITUTIONS, STRUCTURES OF AUTHORITY, AND OFFICIAL HISTORY.

HIS WAS A VIRTUOSO, AUTEURIST VERSION OF A KIND OF REACTIONARY FILMMAKING THAT DID NOT LACK FOR OTHER EXAMPLES THROUGHOUT THE '70s: DISASTER, VIGILANTE, AND WAR MOVIES (*THE GREEN BERETS*) EXTOLLING THE VIRTUES OF AMERICAN ENGAGEMENT IN SOUTHEAST ASIA.

UNLIKE MOST NEW HOLLYWOOD FILMMAKERS, FRIEDKIN DID NOT SEE THE WORLD AS BEING DIVIDED INTO IDENTIFIABLE CAMPS—NOR WAS HE CONCERNED WITH SITUATING HIMSELF AMONG THEM.

WILLIAM FRIEDKIN IS A SUBVERSIVE, UNCOMPROMISING DIRECTOR, NO DOUBT AMONG THE MOST RADICAL AMERICAN FILM HAS EVER KNOWN. HIS MOVIES ALL LIVE ON THE EDGE, EXPLORING THE LIMITS, WALKING THE LINE BETWEEN GOOD AND EVIL—HIS ONLY TRUE SUBJECT OF COURSE (HOW TO SPEAK OF ONE WITHOUT THE OTHER?). BUT HE NEVER COMES DOWN ON ONE SIDE.

FOR FRIEDKIN, THE WORST THING, THE UNTHINKABLE, IS JUST THE PART OF OURSELVES WE HAVEN'T YET DARED LOOK IN THE EYE. IN FRIEDKIN'S UNIVERSE, THERE'S NO GETTING AWAY THROUGH FANTASY, NO HAPPY ESCAPE TO PARALLEL UNIVERSES OR PRIVATE WORLDS: THE WORLD IS ULTRA-REAL AND VIOLENT, LITERAL, IN THE IMAGE OF MAN AND HIS MADNESS. HIS TYPICALLY DOCUMENTARY STYLE CAN NEVER LONG WITHSTAND THE INSANE VISIONS THAT ASSAIL HIS CHARACTERS AND, INEVITABLY, HIS FILMS DRIFT TOWARD BECOMING DARK, HALLUCINATORY DREAMS.

COPPOLA: THE MOGUL

BACK THEN, A YOUNG GUY MAKING A FEATURE-LENGTH FILM? UNHEARD OF! I WAS THE FIRST!

IT IS, OF COURSE, COPPOLA WHO BEST EMBODIES THE DREAMS OF POWER AND THE CRUSHING DISILLUSION OF THIS GENERATION.

IN HIS BOOK *EASY RIDERS, RAGING BULLS*, PETER BISKIND PAINTS A PORTRAIT—PART MONSTER, PART MAN—OF A RAVING MEGALOMANIAC WHO, VERY EARLY ON, WAS CROWNED WITH AN AURA OF PRESTIGE, THANKS TO *YOU'RE A BIG BOY NOW* (1966).

FRANCIS WAS OUR IDOL. IF WE COULD MEET FRANCIS, THAT WAS AS CLOSE AS TO GOD AS ONE COULD GET.

MARGOT KIDDER

IN 1969, COPPOLA AND LUCAS FOUNDED THEIR OWN PRODUCTION COMPANY, AMERICAN ZOETROPE, HEADQUARTERED IN SAN FRANCISCO.

OVER THE COURSE OF THE 1970S, IT WOULD GO ON TO PRODUCE *THE RAIN PEOPLE*, *THX 1138* (LUCAS'S FIRST FILM), *THE CONVERSATION* (1974), AND *APOCALYPSE NOW*.

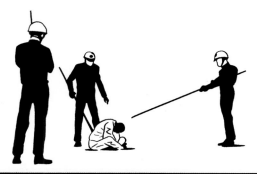

THE FILM THAT SHOT COPPOLA'S CAREER INTO THE STRATOSPHERE WAS, OF COURSE, 1972'S *THE GODFATHER*.

AFTER THE FILM'S CRITICAL AND COMMERCIAL SUCCESS, COPPOLA WAS ADMIRED AND RESPECTED, FAR MORE SO THAN HE COULD'VE IMAGINED A FEW YEARS EARLIER. HE HAD SUCCEEDED AT THE HARDEST POSSIBLE THING IN HOLLYWOOD: BEING RECOGNIZED AS A DIRECTOR ABLE TO FILL SEATS BUT ALSO AS AN AUTEUR, THUS FULFILLING THE TWIN DREAMS OF MOST NEW HOLLYWOOD DIRECTORS.

INDEED, THESE DIRECTORS— UNLIKE THEIR EUROPEAN NEW WAVE COUNTERPARTS WHO WISHED TO STAY OUTSIDE A SYSTEM THEY REJECTED— WANTED TO CONQUER THE CINEMATIC MECCA, TO STORM THE HOLLYWOOD CITADEL AND IMPOSE THEIR VISION, THEIR WAY OF MAKING MOVIES, UPON IT.

AT THE TIME, GEORGE LUCAS, DESCRIBED AS AN INFLEXIBLE AND INTROVERTED MAN, WAS COPPOLA'S PROTÉGÉ (FOR A LONG TIME, COPPOLA WANTED HIM TO SHOOT *APOCALYPSE NOW*).

BUT A FEW YEARS LATER, WHEN LUCAS AND SPIELBERG BECAME TWO OF THE MOST POWERFUL FIGURES IN HOLLYWOOD, COPPOLA, THEN ON THE WANE, WOULD WAIT A LONG TIME FOR HIS "FRIEND" TO RETURN THE FAVOR.

HE NEVER SAW IT COMING.

THE MOOD IN THE AIR

ALL THE STANDARDS AMERICAN SOCIETY HAD LIVED BY UP UNTIL THE 1960S WERE CALLED INTO QUESTION: WHAT WERE PATRIOTISM, BRAVERY, JUSTICE, VIRTUE, EVIL? AUDIENCES FOR NEW HOLLYWOOD FILMS NOW WANTED MOVIES THAT RESEMBLED THEIR LIVES; THEY WANTED TO SEE THEMSELVES AND THE WORLD THEY LIVED IN REPRESENTED UP ON SCREEN.

THEY NO LONGER WANTED THAT DISTANCE, THAT GLAMOROUS VISION HOLLYWOOD AND THE STUDIOS HAD MANUFACTURED UP TILL THEN. SHOW US THE WORLD AS IT IS, AND NOT AS YOU WANT IT TO BE!

INFLUENCES ON THIS GENERATION OF FILMMAKERS INCLUDED: ROSSELLINI, FELLINI, ANTONIONI, BERGMAN, BUÑUEL, GODARD, DE SICA, VISCONTI... *LA DOLCE VITA* WAS A HUGE HIT ON CALIFORNIA CAMPUSES. THROUGH THESE FILMS, PEOPLE DISCOVERED NEW WAYS OF TELLING STORIES.

TO THEM, EUROPE WAS ANOTHER PLANET. MOVIES WERE SHOT ON LOCATION; ACTORS LOOKED LIKE NORMAL, EVEN EVERYDAY PEOPLE; THERE WAS TOTAL TONAL FREEDOM. THE WORLD WAS VIBRANT AND QUIVERING RIGHT UP THERE, ON SCREEN. IN THIS LIGHT, EAST COAST FILMMAKER JOHN CASSAVETES WAS A PIONEER WITH *SHADOWS* IN 1958.

A FEW THINGS NEW HOLLYWOOD FILMS HAD IN COMMON:

THEY QUESTIONED OFFICIAL HISTORIES AND ITS GREAT FIGURES.

THEY WERE EXPLICIT AND DIRECT ABOUT SEX AND VIOLENCE.

THEY WERE CHRONICALLY, CATEGORICALLY SKEPTICAL OF ALL FORMS OF AUTHORITY AND POWER.

THEY PLAYED AROUND WITH PLOTS AND CHRONOLOGY (*EASY RIDER*, MIKE NICHOLS' *CATCH-22*).

THEY HAD A DOCUMENTARY, REALISTIC DIMENSION: DRUGS IN *PANIC AT NEEDLE PARK* (THE FIRST TIME AUDIENCES SAW SOMEONE SHOOT UP ON SCREEN).

THEY WERE SYMPATHETIC TO OUTSIDERS AND OUTCASTS (NATIVE AMERICANS, BLACKS, MEXICANS, POOR PEOPLE, MONSTERS...)

THEY HAD AN ABSURD, TRAGIC, DISENCHANTED TAKE ON THE WORLD, A THOUSAND MILES AWAY FROM THE MAGICAL, EDIFYING ASPECT OF CLASSICAL HOLLYWOOD CINEMA.

THEY WERE CRITICAL OF MYTHS AND THE EFFICACY OF ACTION. CHARACTERS STRUGGLED, BUT IN VAIN; THEY HAD GOALS THEY NEVER REACHED; THEY MADE UP WORLDS THAT THEY ALONE INHABITED (TAXI DRIVER).

THEY MISTRUSTED PATRIARCHAL, MASCULINE, AND FAMILIAL MODELS.

MOST NEW HOLLYWOOD FILMS ALSO ATTACKED TRADITIONAL MASCULINITY.

FAMILY WAS NO LONGER A REFUGE, THE HOME-SWEET-HOME JUDY GARLAND LONGED FOR IN THE WIZARD OF OZ, BUT RATHER A LOCUS OF ANXIETY ONE SOUGHT TO ESCAPE (THE GRADUATE, COPPOLA'S THE RAIN PEOPLE), A PLACE OF EVIL (FOR INSTANCE, IN DE PALMA'S CARRIE).

GENRES WERE DECONSTRUCTED AND CRITICALLY REVISED.

THERE WAS A TIME, IN HOLLYWOOD, WHEN CENSORSHIP WAS THE RULE OF THE DAY. IN FACT, IT STEMMED FROM THE MAJOR STUDIO HEADS THEMSELVES WHO, FACED WITH THE FINANCIAL THREAT LEVIED AGAINST MOVIES BY PURITAN GROUPS AND OTHER LEAGUES OF VIRTUE, TASKED A CERTAIN WILLIAM HAYS, PRESBYTERIAN AND MEMBER OF THE REPUBLICAN PARTY, WITH DRAFTING A CODE OF MORAL CONDUCT, KNOWN AS THE HAYS CODE.

ESSENTIALLY CENTERED AROUND MORAL ISSUES, THIS CODE OF SELF-CENSORSHIP OUTLAWED A GRAB BAG OF ELEMENTS IN-CLUDING PROSTITUTION, OBSCENITY, BARE MIDRIFFS, CHEST HAIR, AND BLASPHEMY. IN CARTOONS, ANIMALS WERE SUDDENLY BANNED FROM BELLY DANCING.

AT THE TIME, INSPECTORS OF ALL SORTS WOULD DESCEND UPON THE SOUNDSTAG-ES: ONE TO MEASURE THE PLACEMENT, RIGHT DOWN TO THE MILLIMETER, OF A MAN'S HAND ON JEAN HARLOW'S BREAST, ANOTHER—KNOWN AS THE "CLEAVAGE CHECKER"—TO EVALUATE THE EXTENT OF THE DÉCOLLETAGE ON ELIZABETH TAYLOR AND KIM NOVAK.

THE FIRST ARTICLE OF THE CODE: "NO PICTURE SHALL BE PRODUCED THAT WILL LOWER THE MORAL STANDARDS OF THOSE WHO SEE IT. HENCE THE SYMPATHY OF THE AUDIENCE SHOULD NEVER BE THROWN TO THE SIDE OF CRIME, WRONGDOING, EVIL OR SIN."

THE MESSAGE WAS CLEAR: THE CODE WAS A WAR BETWEEN THE COLD FISH UP IN NEW ENGLAND AND THE SWINGING CALI-FORNIANS, THE WATCHDOGS OF UPSTAND-ING MORALITY AND THE SUBVERSIVE FREE SPIRITS OF HOLLYWOOD.

APPROVED
CERTIFICATE

BETTY BOOP BEFORE AND AFTER THE CODE.

THE HAYS CODE WAS IMPLEMENTED IN 1934, AND OVER THE YEARS, PROGRESSIVELY STRIPPED OF ITS PROHIBITIONS, BEFORE BEING DEFINITELY REPLACED IN 1966 BY A SYSTEM OF FILM RATINGS THAT, GIVE OR TAKE A FEW ADJUSTMENTS, HAS SURVIVED TILL THIS DAY.

THE RETURN OF THE 1930s

MANY FILMS OF THE 1970S (BOXCAR BERTHA, THIEVES LIKE US, BONNE AND CLYDE, HARD TIMES, PAPER MOON, CHINATOWN, ETC.) HEARKENED BACK TOWARDS THE 1930S, AS IF TO RENEW A LOST CONNECTION, OR REVIVE AN OLD MODEL.

HYPOTHESIS: WHAT IF AMERICAN MOVIES IN THE 1970S RECONNECTED WITH THIS STRANGE PERIOD IN AMERICAN FILM FROM 1929-1934, KNOWN AS THE "PRE-CODE" ERA—DURING WHICH THE HAYS CODE WAS BEING FORMULATED BUT HAD NOT YET BEEN APPLIED—BECAUSE FILMMAKERS AND PRODUCERS BACK THEN WERE FREE TO FOLLOW THEIR OCCASIONALLY STRIKING AND ALWAYS DARING WHIMS?

DURING THOSE FOUR DREAMLIKE YEARS, HOLLYWOOD PRODUCED SCORES OF BIZARRE AND INNOVATIVE FILMS, CASTING A HARSH, BRUTAL, AND OFTEN IRONIC EYE ON THE REALITIES OF AMERICAN POLITICS AND SOCIETY. SO MUCH REALITY, AND SO MANY VISIONARY DREAMS, THAT THE CODE, COMING INTO EFFECT IN 1934, PUT A LID ON IT ALL THE WAY UNTIL 1968, WHEN IT WAS REPEALED.

When it comes to killing ...Mama knows best!

AMERICA IN THE 30'S WAS A FREE COUNTRY.

WE FELT A ROMANTIC KIND OF KINSHIP WITH THE 1930S. ALL THE YOUNG DIRECTORS HAD A GREAT DEAL OF RESPECT FOR FILMMAKERS OF THAT ERA, MUCH MORE SO THAN FOR 1950S FILMMAKERS, FOR INSTANCE. PLUS, IT WAS OUR PARENTS' ERA, SO IT WAS VERY MUCH ALIVE IN THE MINDS OF PEOPLE OF MY GENERATION. IT WAS LIKE THE '60S WOULD BE FOR OUR CHILDREN.

WALTER HILL

MATRIX 1:
KISS ME DEADLY,
ROBERT ALDRICH, 1956.

EN QU4TRIEME VITESSE

ROBERT ALDRICH WAS, WITHOUT A DOUBT, ONE OF THE FIRST AMERICAN DIRECTORS WHO, AS EARLY AS THE OUTSET OF THE 1950S, IN SUCH FILMS AS *VERA CRUZ* AND *KISS ME DEADLY*, ENSURED THE TRANSITION FROM CLASSICAL HOLLYWOOD TO SELF-CRITICAL MODERNITY, INFUSING HIS EVERY SHOT WITH INCREDIBLE ENERGY AND BRUTALITY THAT LENT A TOUCH OF HYSTERIA TO WESTERNS, FILM NOIR, THRILLERS, AND HIS OWN FAVORITE GENRE: THE WAR FILM.

FOR ALDRICH'S HEROES, THE WORLD WAS AN ARENA AND THE ONLY GOAL SURVIVAL, NO HOLDS BARRED. IDEALISTS HAD NO PLACE HERE: THE SYSTEM CHEWED THEM UP, LIKE JACK PALANCE, AN ACTOR THE HOLLYWOOD INDUSTRY DESTROYS IN *THE BIG KNIFE*, OR BURT REYNOLDS, A DISILLUSIONED COP IN *HUSTLE*.

MATRIX 2:
INVASION OF THE BODY SNATCHERS,
DON SIEGEL, 1956.

THE PREMISE: ONE BY ONE, THE PEOPLE OF A SMALL CALIFORNIA TOWN ARE REPLACED BY EMOTIONLESS DOUBLES. A PSYCHIATRIST INVESTIGATES THE PHENOMENON.

THE THEME: A FILM THAT FORESHADOWED THE REST OF DON SIEGEL'S OEUVRE, OBSESSED WITH THE FEAR THAT HUMAN BEINGS WOULD BE FORMATTED AND PROGRAMMED OUT OF EXISTENCE.

WHAT IS A BODY SNATCHER? AN ENTITY OF VEGETABLE ORIGIN THAT DUPLICATES, THEN REPLACES, A LIVING ORGANISM WITH AN EXACT REPLICA. THE RESULTING COPY IS IDENTICAL IN EVERY WAY.

AS IF EMERGING FROM A WAKING DREAM, THE PEOPLE OF THE QUIET LITTLE CAPRAESQUE TOWN OF SANTA MIRA ARE REBORN AS THEMSELVES, ALL JUST AS THEY WERE AND YET NOW DEFINITIVELY OTHER.

NO LONGER A COMMUNITY OF DISCRETE BEINGS WITH THEIR OWN CONFLICTS AND RELATIONSHIPS, THEY ARE INSTEAD AN UNDIFFERENTIATED MASS WITHOUT INDIVIDUAL SUBJECTS: THE HELL OF SAMENESS.

INVASION OF THE BODY SNATCHERS

THE FILM CONTAINS, IN EMBRYO, A FEW ISSUES THAT WOULD PROVE CENTRAL TO NEW HOLLYWOOD MOVIES: PARANOIA (IT'S THE GRANDFATHER OF ALL CONSPIRACY THRILLERS), THE THREAT OF SIMULACRA (MOST ZOMBIE, ANDROID, AND ROBOT FILMS OF THE ERA, FROM *WESTWORLD* TO *BLADE RUNNER*, REVOLVED AROUND REDEFINING HUMANITY).

IN NEW HOLLYWOOD, THERE WOULD BE MOVIES ABOUT PEOPLE DISAPPEARING, MOVIES ABOUT THE COLDNESS OF TECHNOLOGICAL VIOLENCE (THE SIEGEL WAY), AND MOVIES ABOUT THE IMPLOSION AND/OR EXPLOSION OF UNCONTROLLABLE VIOLENCE (THE ALDRICH WAY).

THE SEARCHERS

YOUNG DEBBIE IS KIDNAPPED BY THE COMANCHES. AFTER FIVE YEARS OF SEARCHING FOR HER, HER UNCLE ETHAN EDWARDS (JOHN WAYNE) AND MARTIN PAWLEY FINALLY PICK UP THE TRAIL OF SCAR, THE INDIAN CHIEF WHO ABDUCTED HER, AND DEBBIE, WHO HAS SINCE BECOME ONE OF HIS (FOUR) SQUAWS.

DEBBIE RETURNS IN THE BACKGROUND IN THE MIDDLE OF THIS SHOT, WHICH NO DOUBT INAUGURATED A NEW RELATIONSHIP BETWEEN AMERICAN MOVIES AND DEPTH OF FIELD.

SOMETHING DECISIVE PLAYED OUT IN THIS SHOT.

FOR FORD, OF COURSE—IT MARKED THE BEGINNING OF DISILLUSION AND THE RETURN OF THE REPRESSED—BUT ALSO FOR AMERICAN CINEMA, WHICH WOULD RADICALLY RETHINK THE RELATIONSHIPS BETWEEN WHAT IS ONSCREEN AND OFF. IN A NUTSHELL: IT DEACTIVATED THE LATTER WHILE RENDERING THE FORMER AMBIGUOUS.

THE CAPTIVITY NARRATIVE IN FORD'S FILM BECAME ONE OF THE BURIED MATRICES FOR A GOOD NUMBER OF NEW HOLLYWOOD FILMS, FROM *TAXI DRIVER* TO *THE DEER HUNTER*.

WHAT TO DO, NOW THAT WHAT IS ONSCREEN (THE TERRITORY OF THE SELF) AND OFFSCREEN (THE TERRITORY OF THE OTHER) ARE CONTAINED WITHIN A SINGLE BODY? HOW TO IDENTIFY THE FOREIGN ELEMENT IN AN APPROACHING FIGURE THAT LOOKS JUST LIKE US? IS DEBBIE WHITE? COMANCHE? A BIT OF BOTH? HOW MUCH OF EACH?

THIS QUESTION, WHICH *THE SEARCHERS* INTUITED AND *TWO RODE TOGETHER* REWORKED, WOULD INFORM THE VERY ESSENCE OF POST-1968 HORROR MOVIES.

WHETHER THEY FEATURED MONSTERS (IN *NIGHT OF THE LIVING DEAD*, THE FIRST ZOMBIE TO APPEAR IN THE GRAVEYARD DOES SO IN THE BACKGROUND), NATIVE AMERICANS (*WOLFEN*, *THE SHINING*), OR REDNECKS (THE RETURN OF THE PIONEER IN A DISILLUSIONING FORM: SEE HOW THE ENTRANCE OF THE FIRST REDNECK IN *DELIVERANCE* REPRODUCES THE SPATIAL LAYOUT IN FORD'S FILM), ALL THESE FILMS WOULD FAVOR DEPTH OF FIELD OVER OFFSCREEN SPACE, WHICH HAD BEEN RENDERED FORMLESS.

ULTIMATELY, ALL THESE FILMS EMBODIED A CERTAIN AMERICAN PAST, A PAST THAT HAD BEEN PUSHED OFFSCREEN BUT WAS COMING BACK WITH A FURY TO CLAIM ITS RIGHT TO THE FRAME.

DEPTH OF FIELD, SEEN AS A POLITICAL SPACE FOR THE RESURGENCE OF EVERYTHING REPRESSED, CAME TO STAND IN FOR OFFSCREEN SPACE, A ZONE OF RADICAL OTHERNESS (EVIL), WHICH 1970S AMERICA NO LONGER BELIEVED IN.

HORROR IS BACK

THE LATE '60S SAW HORROR FILMS BECOME CONTAMINATED BY THE TECHNIQUES OF REALISM, AND VICE VERSA. MANY REALIST FILMS BORROWED CERTAIN GENRE TROPES (SUPERNATURAL ATMOSPHERE, PARANOID MOOD, IRRUPTION OF GORE), WHILE HORROR MOVIES, WHICH TILL THEN HAD LITTLE USE FOR THE VIRTUES OF REALISM, LEFT THEIR ROOTS BEHIND AND EMBRACED DOCUMENTARY AESTHETICS.

AS A RESULT, 1970S HORROR MOVIES WERE NOT SIMPLY A WHOLESALE DISPLAY OF EVERYTHING THAT HAD BEEN OVERLOOKED OR OBSCURED (A GAME OF HIDE-AND-SEEK FOUNDED ON THE WITHHOLDING OF DESIRE, ELLIPSIS, AND OFFSCREEN SPACE), BUT BECAME A PRIVILEGED AND HYPER-POLITICIZED SPACE WHERE AMERICA CONFRONTED ITS NEW DEMONS.

NIGHT OF THE LIVING DEAD, GEORGE ROMERO, 1968.
GRAINY BLACK AND WHITE (THE FILM WAS SHOT IN 16MM), UNUSUAL AND UNSTABLE COMPOSITIONS, DISTORTED IMAGES, ROUGH EDITING, NO NAME ACTORS, TRIVIAL DETAILS: ROMERO'S FILM HAD ALL THE EARMARKS OF WAR REPORTAGE, STARTING WITH THE SHOOTING STYLE. IMAGES SEEMED CAUGHT ON THE FLY, SUBJECT TO THE VAGARIES OF SOME MONSTROUS EVENT.

NIGHT OF THE LIVING DEAD ABANDONED THE HORROR GENRE'S CODES AND MYTHOLOGICAL MOTIFS, INSTEAD RECYCLING THE DOCUMENTARY AESTHETIC THAT MARKED THE LATE '60S, IN THE SAME WAY THAT *DAWN OF THE DEAD*, TEN YEARS LATER, WOULD DEPICT THE UGLINESS OF SITCOMS AND THE ERA'S TELEVISED REALITY SHOWS. IN THIS WAY, *NIGHT OF THE LIVING DEAD* WAS ABLE TO ECHO NEWS FOOTAGE FROM VIETNAM AS WELL AS PRESIDENT KENNEDY'S GORY ASSASSINATION.

THE ZOMBIE'S ROTTING BODY AMOUNTED TO A SYMBOLIC FIGURE FOR THE DECADE: A LITERAL SYMBOL OF THE DEAD END CONSUMERIST SOCIETY HAD COME TO, AND THE PEOPLE AMERICAN HISTORY HAD BURIED ALIVE. THE REVISIONIST FICTION STORMED THE SCREEN, SPILLING PAST THE EDGES OF THE FRAME...

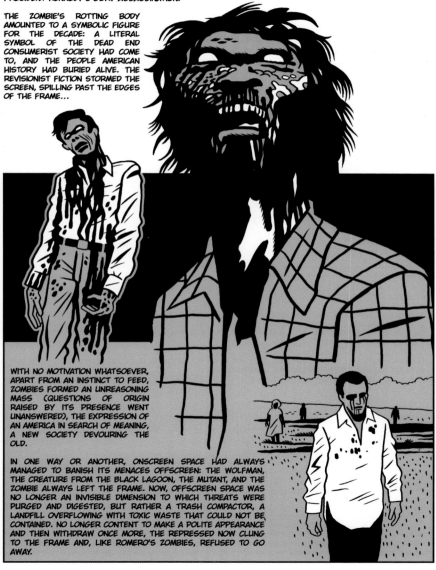

WITH NO MOTIVATION WHATSOEVER, APART FROM AN INSTINCT TO FEED, ZOMBIES FORMED AN UNREASONING MASS (QUESTIONS OF ORIGIN RAISED BY ITS PRESENCE WENT UNANSWERED), THE EXPRESSION OF AN AMERICA IN SEARCH OF MEANING, A NEW SOCIETY DEVOURING THE OLD.

IN ONE WAY OR ANOTHER, ONSCREEN SPACE HAD ALWAYS MANAGED TO BANISH ITS MENACES OFFSCREEN: THE WOLFMAN, THE CREATURE FROM THE BLACK LAGOON, THE MUTANT, AND THE ZOMBIE ALWAYS LEFT THE FRAME. NOW, OFFSCREEN SPACE WAS NO LONGER AN INVISIBLE DIMENSION TO WHICH THREATS WERE PURGED AND DIGESTED, BUT RATHER A TRASH COMPACTOR, A LANDFILL OVERFLOWING WITH TOXIC WASTE THAT COULD NOT BE CONTAINED. NO LONGER CONTENT TO MAKE A POLITE APPEARANCE AND THEN WITHDRAW ONCE MORE, THE REPRESSED NOW CLUNG TO THE FRAME AND, LIKE ROMERO'S ZOMBIES, REFUSED TO GO AWAY.

THE ROAD MOVIE HITS THE ROAD

THE TERM "ROAD MOVIE" BECAME POPULAR IN 1970 AFTER THE RELEASE OF BOB RAFELSON'S *FIVE EASY PIECES* AS A WAY OF DESCRIBING THE GROUP OF FILMS THAT, SINCE *EASY RIDER* IN THE LATE '60S, HAD USED THE ROAD AS A NARRATIVE BACKBONE.

IN 1971, RICHARD SARAFIAN MADE *VANISHING POINT*, DOUBTLESS THE PARAGON OF ALL ROAD MOVIES, SINCE THE HYBRID GENRE INSISTS LESS ON THE ROAD ITSELF THAN ON THE JOURNEY OF AN INDIVIDUAL OR GROUP THROUGH AN OFTEN HOSTILE SPACE.

THE ROAD MOVIE WAS AN ODD GENRE: AT ONCE A "SUBGENRE"—A NATURAL DESCENDANT OF THE WESTERN, AND A "SUPERGENRE"—THEMATICALLY COINCIDING WITH THE "CULTURE OF THE OPEN ROAD," ITSELF AN IDEALIZED VERSION OF THE COUNTRY'S HISTORY (FOUNDING MYTHS AND LEGENDS, A VISION OF AMERICA BUILT UP IN BUFFALO BILL'S WILD WEST SHOW AND EARLY WESTERNS).

THE ROAD MOVIE IS, FIRST OF ALL, AN IDEALIZATION: A CONTINUATION OF THE WESTERN'S AMERICAN PROMISE OF SPACE AND INDIVIDUAL FREEDOM "FOR ALL."

IT IS ALSO A SPACE FOR CRITIQUE: HITTING THE ROAD MEANS PICKING UP THE THREAD OF HISTORY (WHICH IS TO SAY, MENDING IT); MOVING FORWARD IN SPACE IS GOING BACK IN TIME. HITTING THE ROAD TO REWRITE HISTORY SO THAT, THIS TIME, NO ONE GETS LEFT BY THE WAYSIDE (MARTYRS AND THE PEOPLE AMERICAN HISTORY HAS FORGOTTEN).

IN OTHER WORDS, IT IS RECONNECTING WITH THE DRIVE TO CONQUER, REMAKING AMERICAN HISTORY, BUT WITHOUT VIOLENCE: "REGENERATION WITHOUT VIOLENCE."

THE RESULT IS A BOOMERANG EFFECT. INSTEAD OF PERPETRATING VIOLENCE (*EASY RIDER'S* PACIFIST BIKERS), VIOLENCE IS PERPETRATED UPON THOSE WHO TRAVEL THE ROAD. COUNTLESS CATASTROPHIC ENDS AWAIT THEM. *EASY RIDER*, MICHAEL CIMINO'S *THUNDERBOLT AND LIGHTFOOT*, MARTIN SCORSESE'S *BOXCAR BERTHA*, MONTE HELLMAN'S *TWO-LANE BLACKTOP*: WAS THIS THE DEATH OF THE HAPPY ENDING?

HISTORICALLY SPEAKING, THE ROAD MOVIE'S DESIRE FOR WILDERNESS WAS BORN TOO LATE, COMING AS IT DID AFTER THE CREATION OF THE INTERSTATE HIGHWAY AND NATIONAL PARK SYSTEMS, AND THE PARCELING OF TERRITORY. THAT WAS ITS CURSE.

BLACK HOLLYWOOD

THE TIME: THE LATE 1960S. AFTER A FEW SHORTS SHOT IN SAN FRANCISCO, A HANDFUL OF NOVELS WRITTEN IN FRENCH, A BRIEF CAREER AS A REPORTER (*FRANCE-OBSERVATEUR* AND *HARA-KIRI*), A FILM (*THE STORY OF A THREE-DAY PASS*, 1968), AND A BIG STUDIO HIT (*WATERMELON MAN*) THAT INSURED HIM A CERTAIN COMFORT, MELVIN VAN PEEBLES RAISED $100,000 AND LAUNCHED THE PRODUCTION OF *SWEET SWEETBACK'S BAADASSSSS SONG*. IN WATTS, AWAY FROM STUDIO INFLUENCE, HE SHOT WHAT WOULD BECOME THE MANIFESTO OF AFRICAN-AMERICAN CINEMA.

SWEET SWEETBACK

A film of
MELVIN VAN PEEBLES

NON-PROFESSIONAL ACTORS FROM LOS ANGELES' BLACK COMMUNITY, A FEW DEBAUCHED FILM TECHS FROM THE PORN INDUSTRY (BOB MAXWELL, THE DP ON *DEEP THROAT*), A DOCUMENTARY STYLE, AND A FEW BRILLIANT MARKETING IDEAS (AN ORIGINAL SOUNDTRACK BY A THEN-UNKNOWN GROUP, EARTH, WIND, AND FIRE), *SWEET SWEETBACK* WAS AN ARTISTIC AS WELL AS FINANCIAL ADVENTURE.

YOU BLED MY MOMMA — YOU BLED MY POPPA — BUT YOU WONT BLEED ME

GONE WERE THE DAYS OF THE "GOOD NEGRO," WHERE THE SUCCESSFULLY INTEGRATED BLACK MAN WAS ESSENTIALLY WHITE—IN SHORT, SIDNEY POITIER IN *GUESS WHO'S COMING TO DINNER?* FOR VAN PEEBLES, THE TIME HAD COME TO AFFIRM HIS OWN IDENTITY, AND IT HAD A NAME: SWEETBACK, THE BLACK GIGOLO, PLAYED BY THE DIRECTOR HIMSELF, AND HOUNDED BY THE POLICE FOR A MURDER HE DIDN'T COMMIT.

RATED BY AN **X** ALL-WHITE JURY

SWEET SWEETBACK'S WAS A POPULAR AND POLITICALLY ENGAGED FILM, ENTERTAINING AND MILITANT, EXPERIMENTAL AND GENRE. AUDIENCES SAW IT FOR WHAT IT WAS (\$45 MILLION AT THE BOX OFFICE). *SWEET SWEETBACK'S BAADASSSSS SONG* WOULD CHANGE THE FACE OF AFRICAN-AMERICAN CINEMA AND OPEN STUDIO DOORS TO FILMMAKERS LIKE SPIKE LEE, JOHN SINGLETON, AND THE HUGHES BROTHERS.

BUT IT WAS ALSO THE BEGINNING OF A VERY POPULAR TREND (EVEN IF PEEBLES REFUSED TO ACKNOWLEDGE THE RELATION): *BLAXPLOITATION.*

THE THEME TO *SHAFT*, A WORLDWIDE HIT COMPOSED BY ISAAC HAYES IN 1971 FOR GORDON PARKS' FILM OF THE SAME NAME, INSTANTLY BECAME THE ANTHEM OF BLAXPLOITATION, THAT GENRE MADE BY AND FOR AFRICAN-AMERICAN AUDIENCES IN THE EARLY '70S: COOL, VIOLENT, SENSUAL URBAN THRILLERS, JUST LIKE DETECTIVE SHAFT HIMSELF.

BLAXPLOITATION HAD ITS ICONS—JIM KELLY, PAM GRIER, FRED WILLIAMSON—AND ITS HIT FILMS, BUT ABOVE ALL, IT FEATURED INCREDIBLE SOUNDTRACKS FROM THE BIGGEST BLACK MUSICIANS OF THE DAY, FROM JAMES BROWN TO MARVIN GAYE, HERBIE HANCOCK TO CURTIS MAYFIELD.

MOVIES HAD ALWAYS BEEN QUICK TO HEAL THE NATION'S WOUNDS—WHETHER THE FATE OF THE NATIVE AMERICANS OR THE VIETNAM WAR—QUICK TO MEND AND RE-EVALUATE ITS HISTORY IN FILM AND FICTION. HOWEVER, THE ISSUES OF SLAVERY AND THE TREATMENT OF AFRICAN-AMERICANS WERE LONG CONSIDERED A BLIND SPOT, A SENSITIVE TOPIC FOR AMERICAN CINEMA.

1865: THE CIVIL WAR ENDS AND SLAVERY IS ABOLISHED. BUT BLACKS IN THE SOUTHERN STATES ARE STILL CALLED "NEGROES," A PERSECUTED SUBCLASS OF HUMANITY.

AN SO BEGINS THE ERA OF SEGREGATION AND THE LAMENTABLE JIM CROW LAWS, WHICH LAST ALMOST 80 YEARS: WHITES LIVE IN FEAR OF MISCEGENATION AND COHABITATION, WHILE BLACKS LIVE IN FEAR OF A TERRIFYINGLY RACIST AND CAPRICIOUS JUSTICE SYSTEM. MEANWHILE, WHAT'S HAPPENING IN HOLLYWOOD?

DOUBTLESS IT ALL GOES BACK TO GRIFFITH'S *BIRTH OF A NATION*, THE FIRST GREAT ACT OF AMERICAN CINEMA, AND CORNERSTONE CRIME TO A HISTORY THAT HOLLYWOOD WILL SPEND DECADES TRYING TO RIGHT.

WITH THIS EPIC, WHICH PRAISES THE ACTIONS OF THE KKK AND MAKES BLACK PEOPLE LOOK RIDICULOUS, HOLLYWOOD FALLS INTO A LONGSTANDING HABIT OF RACISM THAT WILL MARK MOST MOVIES PRODUCED UNTIL THE MID-60S.

THIS IS RACISM AS A MATTER-OF-COURSE. DESPITE ITSELF, 1927'S *THE JAZZ SINGER* ONLY MAKES IT WORSE, WHAT WITH ITS YOUNG JEW FROM A NEW YORK GHETTO PERFORMING IN BLACKFACE (AS IN A MINSTREL SHOW) TO FURTHER HIS CAREER IN JAZZ. TWO YEARS LATER, KING VIDOR WILL POLARIZE OPINIONS BY MAKING *HALLELUJAH*, THE FIRST HOLLYWOOD FILM TO FEATURE AN ALL-BLACK CAST.

IN THE 1930S AND '40S, A FEW MOVIES ADDRESSED RACE ISSUES, BUT IN A ROUNDABOUT WAY, FROM INSIDE AN INDUSTRY WHERE AFRICAN-AMERICAN HISTORY WAS STILL TABOO.

AMONG THE FILMS TO RAISE A DISSENTING VOICE WERE JOHN STAHL'S 1934 *IMITATION OF LIFE*, ITS MAGNIFICENT 1959 REMAKE BY DOUGLAS SIRK, AND ARCHIE MAYO'S 1937 *BLACK LEGION*, IN WHICH HUMPHREY BOGART PLAYED A WORKER WHO SUCCUMBS TO THE CALL OF THE KU KLUX KLAN.

STARTING IN THE LATE 1940S, THE FIRST OPENLY ANTI-RACIST FILMS SAW THE LIGHT OF DAY IN HOLLYWOOD: *THE WORLD, THE FLESH, AND THE DEVIL, CARMEN JONES*, RAOUL WALSH'S *BAND OF ANGELS*, ROBERT WISE'S *ODDS AGAINST TOMORROW* WITH HARRY BELAFONTE, AND IN 1963, ROBERT MULLIGAN'S *TO KILL A MOCKINGBIRD*.

BUT MALCOLM X'S MILITANT SPEECHES, MARTIN LUTHER KING'S CALL TO PACIFISM, THE CIVIL RIGHTS MOVEMENT, AND THE BIRTH OF BLACK POWER SOON OPENED THE FLOODGATES.

AMERICA—AND AS A RESULT, HOLLYWOOD—FINALLY SEEMED READY TO FACE THE TRUTH ABOUT AFRICAN-AMERICANS' PAINFUL PAST. BLACK PEOPLE BECAME HEROES, AT LEAST IN BLAXPLOITATION; HERBERT BIBERMAN MADE *SLAVES*, AND JOSEPH SARGENT EVEN CAST BLACK ACTOR JAMES EARL JONES AS THE PRESIDENT OF THE UNITED STATES IN *THE MAN* IN 1972.

THE FOLLOWING YEAR, RICHARD FLEISCHER DELIVERED *MANDINGO*, THE VIOLENT UNDERSIDE TO DAILY LIFE AS DEPICTED IN *GONE WITH THE WIND*, AND A FILM TO WHICH QUENTIN TARANTINO'S *DJANGO* IS INDEBTED.

BULLITT. FILMED IN 1968, PETER YATES' FILM MARKED A PIVOTAL MOMENT IN THE HISTORY OF THE AMERICAN THRILLER FOR AT LEAST TWO REASONS:

1. FRANK BULLITT, AN HONEST COP FORCED TO GO OUTSIDE THE LAW TO DO HIS JOB, PAVED THE WAY FOR THE NEW '70S COP MOVIE. *MADIGAN*, DIRTY HARRY, AND POPEYE DOYLE (*THE FRENCH CONNECTION*) WOULD FOLLOW IN ITS FOOTSTEPS. ABRUPT VIOLENCE, INSTITUTIONAL CORRUPTION... WATERGATE AMERICA WAS REARING ITS UGLY HEAD.

2. WITH ITS MAIN CHASE SEQUENCE, *BULLITT* INVENTED AND CEMENTED THE CONVENTIONS OF THE MODERN ACTION MOVIE. CAR CHASES BECAME THE STAR ATTRACTION, A REQUIRED ELEMENT.

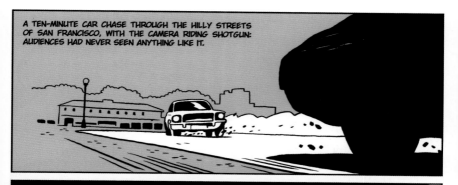

A TEN-MINUTE CAR CHASE THROUGH THE HILLY STREETS OF SAN FRANCISCO, WITH THE CAMERA RIDING SHOTGUN: AUDIENCES HAD NEVER SEEN ANYTHING LIKE IT.

WITH THIS SHOW-STOPPING SET PIECE, THE STORY GROUND TO A HALT AND THE GLEAMING MACHINE OF PURE CINEMA TOOK OVER, RUNNING AT TOP SPEED.

AUGUST 1969: CHARLES MANSON AND THE MURDER OF SHARON TATE

THE IMAGE OF THE HIPPIE—TILL THEN SEEN AS HARMLESS, EVEN LIKABLE—WAS TRANSFORMED.

DENNIS HOPPER: "I THINK CHARLES MANSON DID MORE DAMAGE TO THE HIPPIES AND THE PEACE AND LOVE MOVEMENT THAN ANYONE ELSE. BEFORE HE CAME ALONG, THE HIPPIE MOVEMENT WAS A VERY POSITIVE THING, AT LEAST FOR ME. MANSON CHANGED ALL THAT. HIS WAS THE MOVEMENT'S FIRST ACT OF INDESCRIBABLE VIOLENCE."

PETER FONDA: "THE TERRIBLE THING ABOUT MANSON WAS THAT HE WASN'T A HIPPIE. HE TOOK THEIR IMAGE HOSTAGE, BUT NOT THEIR HEART. THAT WAS A TRULY DIABOLICAL THING.

"ALL HE WANTED WAS TO START WARS AND RACIST CONFLICTS. NOT AGAINST THE ESTABLISHMENT, BUT AGAINST BLACKS, MINORITIES, ETC.

"NOTHING TO DO WITH THE HIPPIE IDEAL. TO US, 'N—' WAS AN UNTHINKABLE WORD, JUST NOT ALLOWED."

BUT BEFORE MANSON THE MURDERER WAS FOUND OUT, THE TRUE MOMENT WHEN COUNTERCULTURAL IDEALS FELL FROM GRACE WAS THE ROLLING STONES CONCERT AT ALTAMONT SPEEDWAY NEAR SAN FRANCISCO ON DECEMBER 5, 1969. WHEN THE HELL'S ANGELS KILLED MEREDITH HUNTER, IT WAS THE END OF THE END. THE HIPPIES HAD (ALREADY) BECOME ZOMBIES.

WHEN A NAKED MAN IS CHASING A WOMAN THROUGH AN ALLEY WITH A BUTCHER KNIFE AND A HARD-ON, I FIGURE HE ISN'T OUT COLLECTING FOR THE RED CROSS.

DIRTY HARRY, 1971.

THERE ONCE WAS A TIME—UNLESS WE DREAMED IT ALL UP—WHEN THE NAME OF *CLINT EASTWOOD* ELICITED AT BEST AMUSED DISDAIN, AT WORST ENDURING HATRED FROM LIBERALS OF EVERY STRIPE, WHO SAW HIM AS THE BARD OF BLIND BRUTALITY, THE RETROGRADE AND RACIST WHITE MAN OF THE NIXON YEARS.

AFTER HE AND HIS SLENDER FRAME SAUNTERED THROUGH INSIPID HOLLYWOOD SERIALS, AND THRICE DONNED A PANCHO TO PLAY SERGIO LEONE'S "MAN WITH NO NAME," CLINT EASTWOOD, AT THE AGE OF 41, FINALLY BECAME A SUPERSTAR. AND IT WAS ALL THANKS TO ONE FILM: *DIRTY HARRY*, WHICH HIS MENTOR DON SIEGEL MADE IN 1971.

FOR A LONG TIME, THE NAME "DIRTY HARRY"—THAT IRASCIBLE SAN FRANCISCO COP LIKELIER TO DRAW HIS MAGNUM .44 THAN A PAIR OF CUFFS—WENT WITH THE NAME EASTWOOD LIKE SACCO WENT WITH VANZETTI.

PATIENTLY, IN MOVIE AFTER MOVIE, THE STAR WORKED TO CHANGE HIS IMAGE. IT WAS A LONG WAY TO REDEMPTION: *THE OUTLAW JOSEY WALES, BRONCO BILLY, HONKYTONK MAN, PALE RIDER, BIRD...* ALL THE WAY TILL *UNFORGIVEN*, IN 1992, WHEN THE UNTHINKABLE HAPPENED. IN THE ROLE OF AN AGING COWBOY RELUCTANTLY TAKING UP ARMS ONCE MORE, EASTWOOD EARNED UNIVERSAL ACCLAIM.

IT WOULD BE NAÏVE TO THINK THAT "HIPPIE" MOVIES WON OVER A MAJORITY OF VIEWERS IN 1970S AMERICA.

OVER THE COURSE OF THE '70S, THERE WAS A SERIES OF FILMS THAT, IF NOT OUTRIGHT UNSAVORY, WERE AT ANY RATE LARGELY OVERLOOKED BY AMERICAN (AND FRENCH) CRITICS AT THE TIME. CRITICS WERE BY AND LARGE SUPPORTERS OF THE NEW HOLLYWOOD GENERATION, WHICH BLITHELY (AND OFTEN A BIT NAIVELY) ESPOUSED SO-CALLED PROGRESSIVE IDEOLOGIES: REMAINING OPPOSED TO ALL FORMS OF POWER, SYMPATHETIC TO MINORITIES, AND ADVOCATING SHARING, PSYCHOTROPIC EXPERIENCES, A RETURN TO NATURE...

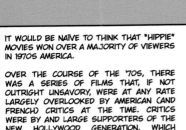

THESE FILMS, WHICH MIGHT BE CALLED "REACTIONARY," DID NOT STAND TOE-TO-TOE IN OPPOSITION TO NEW HOLLYWOOD FILMS SO MUCH AS EXPLORE THEIR PATHOLOGICAL UNDERBELLY.

BY ALL APPEARANCES, THESE FILMS SEEMED TO SET THEMSELVES UP ON THE SIDE OF POWER AND INSTITUTIONS, BUT ONLY TO POINT OUT THEIR IMPOTENCE, PATHOLOGICAL WAYWARDNESS, AND SOMETIMES EXISTENTIAL ABSURDITY.

IN AMERICAN CINEMA OF THE ERA, THESE FILMS WERE THE EQUIVALENT OF WHAT ANTOINE COMPAGNON HAS CALLED THE "ANTI-MODERNS" IN LITERATURE: "THE ANTI-MODERN IS THE REVERSE OF THE MODERN, ITS INTAGLIO, ITS INDISPENSABLE RECESSES, ITS RESERVES AND RESOURCE. WITHOUT ANTI-MODERNITY, MODERNITY WOULD GO RUSHING TOWARD ITS DOOM, FOR THE ANTI-MODERNS ARE THE FREEDOM OF THE MODERNS, OR THE MODERNS PLUS FREEDOM."

WHAT THEY DID, THEN, WAS COUNTERBALANCE THE MASSIVE EMERGENCE OF AN OUTPUT EXTOLLING COUNTERCULTURAL IDEALS AND THE DESIRE FOR CHANGE.

AMONG THE RESPONSES HOLLYWOOD CAME UP WITH—URBAN THRILLERS REVOLVING AROUND REVENGE OR SUMMARY JUSTICE—THE MOST WELL-KNOWN ARE *COOGAN'S BLUFF* (DON SIEGEL, 1968), *DIRTY HARRY* (DON SIEGEL, 1971), AND ABOVE ALL, *DEATH WISH* (MICHAEL WINNER, 1974), THE FILM THAT BEST EXEMPLIFIED THE TREND.

ANOTHER SERIES OF FILMS TACKLING THE SAME THEMES, BUT SET IN RURAL AMERICA, SURFACED IN THE MIDDLE OF THE DECADE. AMONG THE MOST NOTABLE WERE THE *WALKING TALL* TRILOGY (LAUNCHED BY PHIL KARLSON IN 1973) AND *ROLLING THUNDER* (JOHN FLYNN).

THESE MOVIES WERE OFTEN ABOUT SELF-DEFENSE, UNAVOIDABLE RECOURSE TO THE VALUES OF THE OLD WEST, TAKING THE LAW INTO ONE'S OWN HANDS, AND THE IMPOTENCE OF THE JUSTICE SYSTEM.

THESE ANTI-MODERNS OF THE 1970S WERE AT ODDS WITH THE MODERNS OF NEW HOLLYWOOD. OR ELSE THEY WERE MODERNS DESPITE THEMSELVES, RECAL- CITRANT MODERNS, MOVING FORWARD WITH ONE WELL-MEANING EYE ON THE REARVIEW MIRROR AT ALL TIMES.

THEY SPEWED OUT CONSERVATISM AND THE STATUS QUO AS OFTEN AS THEY DID THE BLIND AND DIZZYING MODERNITY OF THE YOUNGER GENERATION. THEY MADE AS MUCH FUN OF RIGID ACADEMICISM AS THEY DID THE ILLUSORY SEDUCTIONS OF NOVELTY AND PROGRESS.

IF NEW HOLLYWOOD FILMS WERE LIBER- TARIAN FILMS, ANTI-MODERN MOVIES WERE MORE LIKE ANARCHIST MOVIES.

NOTHING TO DO BUT CUT AND RUN. WHAT ELSE? WHAT ABOUT THE OLD AMERICAN SOCIAL CUSTOM OF SELF-DEFENSE? IF THE POLICE DON'T DEFEND US, MAYBE WE OUGHT TO DO IT OURSELVES.

WE'RE NOT PIONEERS ANYMORE, DAD.

WHAT ARE WE, JACK? I MEAN, IF WE'RE NOT PIONEERS, WHAT HAVE WE BECOME? WHAT DO YOU CALL PEOPLE WHO, WHEN FACED WITH A CONDITION OF FEAR, DO NOTHING ABOUT IT? THEY JUST RUN AND HIDE.

CIVILISED?

NO.

DEATH WISH NO DOUBT REPRESENTS THE RADICAL VERSION OF A FRACTURE THAT APPEARED IN THE URBAN POLICE THRILLER IN THE '60S AND '70S.

FREED FROM THE SHACKLES OF THE LAW, PAUL KERSEY IS A SIMPLE CITIZEN LAYING DOWN HIS OWN BRAND OF JUSTICE. NEVERTHELESS, HE REMAINS SOMEONE WHO EMBODIED THE DESIRES OF MOST OF THE ERA'S COPS, THE ANTI-SERPICO.

DISASTER AND DISASTER

IN *TAXI DRIVER*, TRAVIS BICKLE'S (ROBERT DE NIRO) IDENTITY CRISIS GETS WORSE AS HIS BODY AND OUTFITS CHANGE. AT THE END OF THE MOVIE, JUST BEFORE THE CARNAGE, WE SEE HIM DRESSED IN AN ARMY JACKET, SPORTING A MOHAWK. A WALKING PARADOX, HE COMBINES THE FEATURES OF A SOLDIER AND A NATIVE AMERICAN, WHICH IN THE LANGUAGE OF A VIETNAM VET MEANS VIETCONG. WE SEE THE VIOLENCE DONE TO THE CLASSICAL STORY, ITS MECHANISMS AND STRUCTURE, AS THE FILM, CLOSELY FOLLOWING THE PSYCHE OF ITS PROTAGONISTS, FINDS ITSELF PULLED IN CONFLICTING DIRECTIONS.

IN AMERICAN CINEMA OF THE 1970S, IT IS FINALLY POSSIBLE NOT TO HAVE CLOSURE. THE TRUTH OF THE WORLD, AND HENCE ITS BEAUTY, IS INVERSELY PROPORTIONAL TO THE ILLUSION OF OUR CONTROL OVER IT. CLASSICAL CINEMA FILLED IN THE BLANKS AND SUPPLIED THE ILLUSION OF A SOLID, COHERENT WORLD.

POST-HOLLYWOODIAN CINEMA, HOWEVER, OCCUPIED THE INTERSTICES OF A REALITY THAT WAS EITHER PROBLEMATIC OR UTTERLY SENSELESS. WHETHER AT A COLLECTIVE LEVEL (SOCIETY) OR A PERSONAL ONE (COUPLES AND ISSUES BETWEEN THE SEXES), DISASTER WAS ONE OF THE MAJOR MOTIFS OF 1970S AMERICAN FILM.

THE FEELING OF A SOCIETY THAT HAD REACHED ITS BREAKING POINT AND COULD ONLY REGRESS TOWARD TOTALITARIAN OR OTHERWISE DEGRADED FORMS CONSTITUTED THE SUBTEXT OF THE PERIOD'S POST-DISASTER MOVIES: *NIGHT OF THE LIVING DEAD, ROLLERBALL, SILENT RUNNING, PLANET OF THE APES, SOYLENT GREEN, LOGAN'S RUN, THX 1138, ZARDOZ, DAWN OF THE DEAD.*

IN 1970S AMERICAN CINEMA, THERE WERE TWO KINDS OF REACTIONS TO THE FILMS OF NEW HOLLYWOOD: ON ONE HAND, ANTI-MODERN MOVIES, AND ON THE OTHER, OUTRIGHT CONSERVATIVE MOVIES ABOUT REVENGE, PUNISHMENT, OR A RETURN TO ORDER.

THE RETURN OF DISASTER MOVIES

A LIST: *THE TOWERING INFERNO, THE POSEIDON ADVENTURE, THE HINDENBURG, AVALANCHE, JAWS,* AND *EARTHQUAKE,* WHICH DEVELOPED A MORE CONSERVATIVE DISCOURSE, CALLING UPON DIVINE AND/OR PRIMITIVE FORCES TO PUNISH AND PURGE THE COUNTERCULTURAL BABYLON OF ITS VICES.

WITH THEIR ROSTERS OF WANING STARS TRYING TO SURVIVE AMIDST CHAOS AND DISPLAYING, WITH EVERY PASSING MINUTE, THE STRENGTH OF STABLE VALUES LIKE COURAGE, LOYALTY, AND HONOR, DISASTER FILMS OF THIS ERA ATTEMPTED A HISTORICAL BRAINWASHING OPERATION, TRYING TO MAKE US BELIEVE THAT WHAT THREATENED AMERICA WASN'T THE VIETNAM WAR, POVERTY, POLITICAL OR FINANCIAL SCANDALS, AND MINORITY RIGHTS, BUT RATHER MOTHER NATURE (FLOODS, HURRICANES, EARTHQUAKES, SHARKS, ETC.) AND THE ARROGANCE OF MEN WHO CHALLENGED THE GODS.

J. HOBERMAN:
"THE DISASTER CYCLE DENIED THAT AMERICANS HAD BECOME JADED OR THAT TRADITIONAL VALUES HAD BROKEN DOWN. THEY INSISTED RATHER, THAT... THESE VALUES PROVED TO BE INTACT... MIDDLE-CLASS VIRTUE PREVAILED... [AS IF] 'THE 1960S NEVER HAPPENED.'"

THE GENRE, WHICH SAW ITS GOLDEN AGE MIDWAY THROUGH THE DECADE, ALSO TRIED TO RESTORE THE ILLUSION OF A PEOPLE ABLE TO FIND THEM-SELVES AND JOIN TOGETHER, SEEING PAST DIFFERENCES OF CULTURE, ETHNICITY, AND CLASS (IN *JAWS*, THE PARTNERSHIP BETWEEN THE OLD BLUE-COLLAR QUINT AND HOOPER, THE YOUNG OCEANOGRAPHER).

THE POSEIDON ADVENTURE

AFTER A DECADE BENEATH THE SIGN OF CHAOS AND COLLAPSE, DISASTER FILMS WOUND THE NATION'S CLOCK BACK FROM THE '70S TO THE '50S. IN THESE MOVIES, SCIENTISTS, LABORERS, SOLDIERS, AND PRIESTS WORKED TOGETHER, UNITED BY A SINGLE DESIRE TO GUN DOWN WHATEVER REPULSIVE CREATURE HAD DARED TRESPASS INTO THE FRAME.

1975. YEAR OF THE HANGOVER

THE MOMENT WHEN THE AUTEURS WERE ESTABLISHED, TOOK OVER THE STUDIOS, AND LURED AUDIENCES BACK INTO THEATRES. THE MID-1970S.

BUT DENNIS HOPPER WAS LOST IN THE HAZE OF DRUGS ON *THE LAST MOVIE*, BOGDANOVICH HAD PUT OUT TWO DUDS (*DAISY MILLER* AND *AT LONG LAST LOVE*), JUST LIKE ALTMAN WITH *BUFFALO BILL AND THE INDIANS* AND ASHBY WITH *BOUND FOR GLORY*. BERT SCHNEIDER HAD TURNED AWAY FROM MOVIEMAKING (HE WAS NOW HELPING THE BLACK PANTHERS, HUEY NEWTON, AND ABBIE HOFFMAN, AND HAD PRODUCED *HEARTS AND MINDS*).

IT WAS A MOMENT WHEN AUDIENCES WERE CHANGING. 1975 WAS THE OFFICIAL END OF THE WAR IN VIETNAM, AND THE BEGINNING OF THE END FOR NEW HOLLYWOOD.

SATURDAY NIGHT FEVER, ROCKY, SUPERMAN... AUDIENCES WERE TIRED OF DEPRESSING, CRITICALLY ACCLAIMED MOVIES. THEY WANTED CONFIDENCE AGAIN, AMERICAN HEROES, VICTORY.

WITH JAWS, ROGER CORMAN REALIZED THAT STUDIOS WERE APPLYING HIS PRINCIPLES FOR EXPLOITATION FILMS BUT WITH MORE MONEY AND TALENT. IT WAS THE END OF AN ERA.

GEORGE LUCAS WAS, WITHOUT A DOUBT, THE FIRST TO SENSE THE CHANGE IN AUDIENCES. IN THE MID-1970S, THEY WERE STARTING TO TIRE OF DARK, VIOLENT, GLOOMY VISIONS THAT HAD FILLED SCREENS SINCE 1968.

AMERICAN GRAFFITI, WHICH HE MADE IN 1973, WAS THE FILM THAT RESULTED FROM HIS PREMONITION.

I DECIDED IT WAS TIME TO MAKE A MOVIE WHERE PEOPLE FELT BETTER COMING OUT OF THE THEATER THAN WHEN THEY WENT IN. I BECAME REALLY AWARE OF THE FACT THAT THE KIDS WERE REALLY LOST... NOW YOU JUST SORT OF SAT THERE AND GOT STONED.

I WANTED TO PRESERVE WHAT A CERTAIN GENERATION OF AMERICANS THOUGHT BEING A TEENAGER WAS REALLY ABOUT—FROM ABOUT 1945 TO 1962.

IN OTHER WORDS, ON THE EVE OF THE VIETNAM WAR AND JFK'S ASSASSINATION.

BY FANTASIZING ABOUT AN INNOCENT AMERICA STRIPPED OF DOUBT, AMERICAN GRAFFITI KISSED THE COUNTERCULTURE GOODBYE AND PAVED THE WAY FOR FILMS OF THE 1980S: A GIGANTIC, AMNESIAC, AND CHILDISH REVIVAL.

IN THE LATE 1970S, MOST OF NEW HOLLYWOOD'S WUNDERKINDS WERE GOING THROUGH A ROUGH PATCH. SCORSESE WAS MAKING NEW YORK, NEW YORK UNDER STRAINED CIRCUMSTANCES, COPPOLA LEFT FOR THE PHILIPPINES TO SHOOT APOCALYPSE NOW, FRIEDKIN WAS IN SOUTH AMERICA FOR SORCERER, AND THE STUDIOS HAD LOST INTEREST IN ASHBY, RAFELSON, AND BOGDANOVICH.

MEANWHILE, LUCAS WAS PUTTING THE FINISHING
TOUCHES ON *STAR WARS* (1977).

THE FINAL ACT OF THE PROPHESIED END OF THE
GOLDEN AGE WAS LUCAS' IDEA FOR LICENSED
MERCHANDISING.

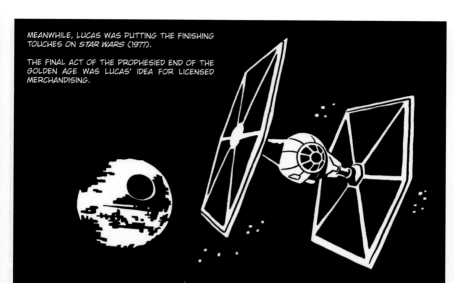

FROM THEN ON, WROTE PETER BISKIND, "IT WOKE UP THE STUDIOS TO
THE POTENTIAL OF MERCHANDISING... ADDING AN INCENTIVE TO REPLACE COMPLEX
CHARACTERS WITH SIMPLE FIGURES THAT COULD BE TURNED INTO TOYS."

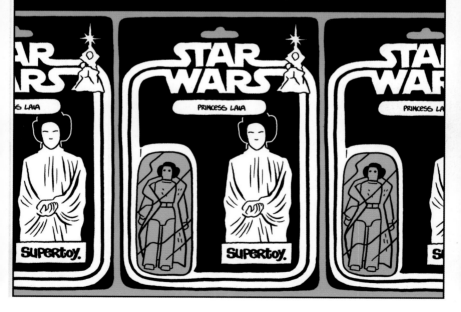

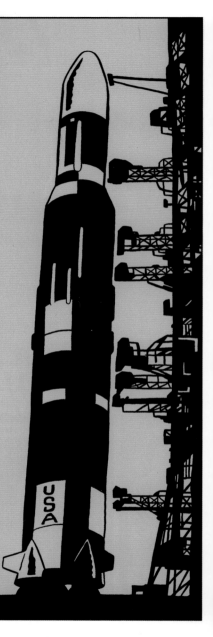

THE BIRTH OF THE BLOCKBUSTER

ETYMOLOGICALLY SPEAKING, THE WORD "BLOCKBUST-ER" IN ENGLISH IS BORROWED FROM MILITARY JARGON AND REFERS TO A LARGE-SCALE BOMB.

LET US BRIEFLY RECALL THREE DATES IN THE HISTO-RY OF THE BLOCKBUSTER, THE MOVIES THAT CALL THE SHOTS IN THE HOLLYWOOD FILM INDUSTRY, WITH BUDGETS REGULARLY IN THE NEIGHBORHOOD OF $200 MILLION

1972. PARAMOUNT SUGGESTS THAT, RATHER THAN STAGGER ITS RELEASE, EXHIBITORS ALL RUN *THE GODFATHER* SIMULTANEOUSLY. THE RESULT? A SHORTENED THEATRICAL RUN AND CRITICAL BUZZ REDUCED TO NIL.

TILL THEN, FILMS HAD COME OUT IN TWO OR THREE STAGES: FIRST NEW YORK, THEN L.A., THEN THE REST OF AMERICA. THIS ALLOWED THEM ALL—ESPE-CIALLY THE MORE ECONOMICALLY FRAGILE ONES—TO HAVE A LONGER RUN, THUS INCREASING CHANCES OF MAKING A PROFIT.

FOR THE RELEASE OF *THE GODFATHER,* FRANK YABLANS, THEN PRESIDENT OF PARAMOUNT, ENVISIONED A NEW MARKETING STRATEGY BASED ON THE SIMULTANEOUS DISTRIBUTION TO ALL EXHIBITORS WHO WANTED A COPY OF THE FILM. 400 SCREENS AT ONCE, $80 MILLION IN PROFITS DURING ITS FIRST RUN. A FIRST.

THE GODFATHER CHANGED THE GAME FOREVER. THE SPECTACLE FILM WAS BORN, ANCESTOR OF THE BLOCKBUSTER AND TODAY'S ESCAPIST TENTPOLES.

UNKNOWINGLY, COPPOLA HAD JUST DESTROYED A SIZABLE CHUNK OF THE INDEPENDENT PRODUCTION FROM WHICH NEW HOLLYWOOD HAD BLOOMED.

1973. WARNER BROS. REPEATED PARAMOUNT'S TACTIC FOR THE RELEASE OF *THE EXORCIST.*

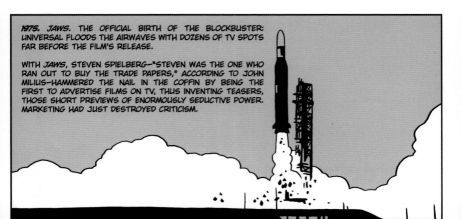

1975. JAWS. THE OFFICIAL BIRTH OF THE BLOCKBUSTER: UNIVERSAL FLOODS THE AIRWAVES WITH DOZENS OF TV SPOTS FAR BEFORE THE FILM'S RELEASE.

WITH *JAWS*, STEVEN SPIELBERG—"STEVEN WAS THE ONE WHO RAN OUT TO BUY THE TRADE PAPERS," ACCORDING TO JOHN MILIUS—HAMMERED THE NAIL IN THE COFFIN BY BEING THE FIRST TO ADVERTISE FILMS ON TV, THUS INVENTING TEASERS, THOSE SHORT PREVIEWS OF ENORMOUSLY SEDUCTIVE POWER. MARKETING HAD JUST DESTROYED CRITICISM.

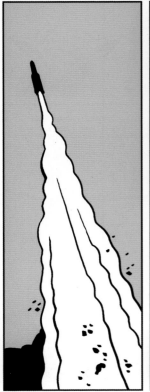

JOHN MILIUS: "THE STUDIOS WANTED TO TURN A QUICK, FAST BUCK—TO PULL OFF SOMETHING LIKE *JAWS*. IN A SENSE, SPIELBERG WAS THE TROJAN HORSE THROUGH WHICH THE STUDIOS BEGAN TO REASSERT THEIR POWER." 1975 MARKED THE END OF AN ERA.

IN 1977, THE LICENSED PRODUCTS THAT ACCOMPANIED THE LAUNCH OF *STAR WARS* INAUGURATED, ONCE AND FOR ALL, THE ERA OF THE BLOCKBUSTER.

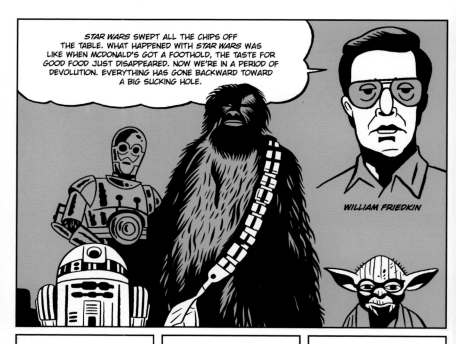

STAR WARS SWEPT ALL THE CHIPS OFF THE TABLE. WHAT HAPPENED WITH *STAR WARS* WAS LIKE WHEN MCDONALD'S GOT A FOOTHOLD, THE TASTE FOR GOOD FOOD JUST DISAPPEARED. NOW WE'RE IN A PERIOD OF DEVOLUTION. EVERYTHING HAS GONE BACKWARD TOWARD A BIG SUCKING HOLE.

WILLIAM FRIEDKIN

THE CHANGE THAT MY GENERATION AND I BELIEVED IN NEVER CAME ABOUT. SUDDENLY, THE BEE GEES SHOWED UP, AND THINGS WERE DIFFERENT. IT WASN'T "I WANT TO START A REVOLUTION" ANYMORE, IT WAS "LOOK, I'VE GOT A PAIR OF NIKES!"

GEORGE ROMERO

THE STUDIO HEADS WERE VERY TRUSTING AND BENEVOLENT TOWARDS US. THAT'S WHY STUDIOS GAVE YOUNG FILMMAKERS SO MUCH FREEDOM IN THE LATE '60S AND THROUGHOUT THE '70S. BUT THEN THEY TOOK THAT FREEDOM BACK.

I THINK THE MOMENT EVERYTHING CHANGED WAS WHEN *STAR WARS* CAME OUT. THAT FILM HAD NOTHING TO DO WITH WHAT THE REST OF US HAD BEEN DOING DURING THE '70S. IT WAS A COMIC BOOK MOVIE.

JOHN BOORMAN

WHEN THE STUDIOS SAW HOW MASSIVELY SUCCESSFUL *STAR WARS* WAS, THEY REALIZED THAT THEIR TARGET AUDIENCES WERE YOUNG BOYS, 14 YEAR OLDS, FANS OF ADVENTURE STORIES AND HEROES THEY COULD IDENTIFY WITH.

THAT WAS WHEN THEY TOOK BACK CONTROL, IN 1977, AND STARTED PRODUCING SERIES OF MOVIES WITH LOTS OF ACTION, BASED ON VERY SIMPLE IDEAS.

MY MOVIE *SORCERER* CAME OUT AT ALMOST THE SAME TIME AS *STAR WARS*, THE FILM THAT CHANGED EVERYTHING IN HOLLYWOOD. *STAR WARS* SOARED TO STRATOSPHERIC HEIGHTS, WHILE *SORCERER* NEVER GOT OFF THE GROUND.

AT THE TIME, I THOUGHT, "WHY ARE SO MANY PEOPLE INTO *STAR WARS*? IT'S A KIDS' MOVIE!"

BUT IT TURNED OUT THAT IT WAS A MOVIE FOR EVERYONE. WHICH *SORCERER* WASN'T. AND FOR GOOD REASON, NO DOUBT: *STAR WARS* BROUGHT YOU GOOD NEWS. EVERYTHING WAS GOING TO BE FINE. GOOD WOULD CONQUER EVIL.

IN *SORCERER*, GOOD DOESN'T CONQUER EVIL. MY FILM DIDN'T HAVE A HAPPY MESSAGE FOR PEOPLE, WHICH WAS IN LINE WITH HOW I THOUGHT OF THINGS BACK THEN.

I DIDN'T REALIZE HOW DIFFERENT THE MESSAGES IN THE TWO MOVIES WERE TILL MUCH LATER.

IN THE 1980s, THE COLOSSAL FINANCIAL FAILURE OF *HEAVEN'S GATE* BROUGHT A SYMBOLIC END TO THE FESTIVITIES. ITS YOUNG DIRECTOR, MICHAEL CIMINO, HAD BEEN ACCLAIMED JUST TWO YEARS EARLIER FOR *THE DEER HUNTER*.

THAT SAME YEAR, REAGAN WAS ELECTED, AND PROCEEDED WITH WHAT JEAN BAUDRILLARD, IN *SIMULACRA AND SIMULATION* (1981), CALLED THE "ANACHRONISTIC RECREATION OF PERFECT WORLD."

SOME DIRECTORS, LIKE SCORSESE AND SPIELBERG, MANAGED TO ADAPT AND RETAIN THEIR SPOTS AT THE PINNACLE OF HOLLYWOOD. THOSE TWO WERE THE BIG WINNERS OF THE NEW HOLLYWOOD GENERATION. OTHERS LIKE COPPOLA, FRIEDKIN, BOGDANOVICH, HELLMAN, ALTMAN, AND HOPPER PURSUED THEIR OWN PATHS, BUT QUIETLY, ON THE FRINGES OF AN INDUSTRY THAT DIDN'T REALLY WANT THEM AROUND ANYMORE. STILL OTHERS VANISHED FROM THE RADAR COMPLETELY (RICHARD SARAFIAN), OR DIED (HAL ASHBY).

YEARS LATER, EACH IN THEIR OWN WAY, COPPOLA AND SCORSESE REVISITED THESE GLORY DAYS AND THEIR BRUTAL DOWNFALL, SMUGGLING PERSONAL THEMES INTO TWO FILMS THAT MAY RETROSPECTIVELY CONSTITUTE THE FINEST COMMENTARIES ON WHAT HAPPENED TO NEW HOLLYWOOD: NAMELY, "WE BLEW IT." WHY AND HOW DID THEY COME TO BLOW IT?

IN *TUCKER* (1988), COPPOLA TRACED THE RISE AND FALL OF A YOUNG DETROIT AUTO ENGINEER SHORTLY AFTER WORLD WAR II. AIDED BY A GROUP OF PASSIONATE CRAFTSMEN, PRESTON TUCKER MANUFACTURES REVOLUTIONARY, INNOVATIVE CARS THAT ENDANGER THE AUTO KINGPINS' MONOPOLY ON THE INDUSTRY. THE MOTOR COMPANIES DO EVERYTHING THEY CAN TO SHUT HIM DOWN.

TUCKER IS CLEARLY A STAND-IN FOR THE MOVIE BRATS WHO, FIFTEEN YEARS AFTER THE PERIOD DEPICTED IN THE MOVIE, WOULD BOLDLY STORM THE HOLLYWOOD CITADEL.

TUCKER LOST, BUT ACTUALLY, HE WON: THE FIFTYSOME CARS THAT CAME OFF HIS PRODUCTION LINE BECAME COLLECTOR'S OBJECTS, FANTASIES, PROTOTYPES THE ENTIRE INDUSTRY STOLE FROM, MODERN-DAY LANDMARKS—JUST LIKE THE FILMS OF NEW HOLLYWOOD.

CASINO (1995) BEGINS IN 1973, AT THE DAWN OF THE GOLDEN AGE OF LAS VEGAS CASINOS. SCORSESE SKETCHES ANOTHER PORTRAIT ALTOGETHER, BARELY BOTHERING TO DISGUISE IT: THE PORTRAIT OF AN ERA HE KNEW FIRSTHAND. THE CHARACTERS THAT ROBERT DE NIRO AND JOE PESCI PLAY SHOW THEMSELVES TO BE INSATIABLE. THEY WANTED INDEPENDENCE WITHOUT HAVING TO ANSWER TO ANYONE.

THEY WANTED TO BRING AN ENTIRE INDUSTRY TO HEEL. THEIR TALENT OPENED THE DOORS OF LAS VEGAS (READ: HOLLYWOOD) TO THEM, BUT THEIR HUBRIS WAS THEIR DOWNFALL. WHO WAS MARTIN SCORSESE TALKING ABOUT, IF NOT HIMSELF, FRANCIS FORD COPPOLA, WILLIAM FRIEDKIN, AND THE WUNDERKIND OF HIS GENERATION?

AT THE END OF THE MOVIE, WE SEE ACE ROTHSTEIN AGAIN, THE FORMER BOSS OF THE TANGIERS, HIS FACE NOW WORN AND LINED. HE HAS BECOME A SIMPLE BOOKMAKER FOR A SMALL CASINO.

HE IS A MAN WHO'S SEEN IT ALL—SUCCESS, EXCESS, HELL, BETRAYAL, WAR—AND NOW HE'S BACK WHERE HE STARTED: ALONE, ON THE FRINGES OF THE SYSTEM, BUT STILL ARMED WITH HIS TALENT. THE END OF NEW HOLLYWOOD DID NOT DESTROY SCORSESE. IT MADE HIM MELANCHOLY.

THE FILMS OF NEW HOLLYWOOD AND THE 1970S REPRESENT
THE FINAL ROMANTIC FRONTIER FOR TODAY'S FANS AND FILMMAKERS.

THEY REMAIN OUR ERA'S POLAR NORTH, A STEADFAST REFERENCE
POINT FOR RECENT HISTORY (THE MEMORY OF KENNEDY'S ASSASSINATION
RETURNING TO HAUNT THE CHAOS OF 9/11, THE VIETNAM WAR
RESURFACING IN IRAQ) AND POP CULTURE.

WHETHER IN THE FILMS OF WES ANDERSON OR MICHAEL MOORE,
JAMES GRAY OR MICHAEL MANN, GUS VAN SANT OR JEFF NICHOLS, QUENTIN
TARANTINO OR DAVID FINCHER—WE ALL PUSH ONWARD WITH ONE EYE ON THE
ROAD AHEAD, AND THE OTHER RIVETED BY THE '70S IN THE REARVIEW
MIRROR, BY THE SPECTACLE OF A GOLDEN AGE MADE ALL THE MORE
DESIRABLE BY THE FACT THAT IT NO LONGER EXISTS.

THE LITTLE BOOK
OF KNOWLEDGE:

NEW HOLLYWOOD